New Models for Creative Giving

Dr. Raymond B. Knudsen is the author of

NEW MODELS FOR FINANCING THE LOCAL CHURCH
STEWARDSHIP ENLISTMENT AND COMMITMENT
DEVELOPING DYNAMIC STEWARDSHIP
NEW MODELS FOR CHURCH ADMINISTRATION
MODELS FOR MINISTRY
THE WORKBOOK
    (A companion volume to all of the above)
THE TRINITY

NEW MODELS
FOR
CREATIVE GIVING

Second Edition

RAYMOND B. KNUDSEN

MOREHOUSE-BARLOW
Wilton

First published by Association Press,
Follett Publishing Company, Chicago

Second edition published by
Morehouse-Barlow Co., Inc.
78 Danbury Road
Wilton, Connecticut 06897

ISBN 0-8192-1370-5

Library of Congress Catalog Card Number 85-061219

Printed in the United States of America

2 4 6 8 10 9 7 5 3 1

Dedicated to my father
FRANKLIN O. KNUDSEN,
and to the memory of my mother
JULIA MARIE KNUDSEN,
who discovered early in
their lives
the fact that
"it is more blessed to give
than to receive"

Contents

Preface

"MISTER, will you give me a dime for a cup of coffee?"

Twenty-five years ago, a person would have answered "Yes" or "No." Now one would respond: "Where can you get a cup of coffee for a dime today?"

The ten-cent cup of coffee has gone the way of the penny postcard. We cannot mail a postcard for one cent, and we cannot buy a cup of coffee for a dime. We know it. We accept it. We have adjusted our lives to it.

When it comes to philanthropy, we simply have not advanced with the times. This does not mean that we are not giving more than we gave when a postcard was a penny and a cup of coffee was one thin dime. It does mean, however, that we have spread our philanthropic dollars so thin that often they neither fill stomachs nor communicate deep concern for needy people. Much of our giving simply does not make a difference!

Perhaps you ought to give more. That is something only you can decide. Whether or not you give more is not the issue. What does your giving accomplish? That is the important question, and if you are among the hundreds of thousands who must reply, "Not very much," it is time to consider some new models for creative giving.

It is exciting to realize that as individuals we sometimes give more than corporations, more than foundations, more than other people. In fact, at times, we give enough to make a real difference.

As individuals, we can make many differences, for there are

many courses we can take in philanthropic giving, and whether or not we use them, we should know what they are and how we can respond to human need and a personal desire to do good in the very best possible way.

My sharing them is a joyful experience. Your using them may be an excellent opportunity.

R.B.K.

ACKNOWLEDGMENT

I would express my sincere gratitude to Robert Roy Wright, Editor for Association Press, in the preparation of the First Edition; and to Stephen S. Wilburn, Editorial Director for Morehouse-Barlow Co., and Raymond B. Knudsen II, President of the National Consultation on Financial Development, for their assistance in the preparation of the Second Edition.

New Models for Creative Giving

1

Our System of Philanthropy
and the Changing Climate

In 1983, Americans gave $65 billion, setting a new record in philanthropy. This represented an increase over the preceding year of $5 billion in spite of changing economic conditions and uncertainty in the business and finance communities.

Sixty-five billion dollars is an impressive sum, especially when we realize that it represents voluntary support. It is not a tax. It is not the result of assessments. It is not required. It is given! It is a product of our system of philanthropy, a system of philanthropy that is growing, and of which all of us—you and I—are a part.

When did philanthropy begin? No one knows for sure, but a single sentence of Jesus' seemed so out-of-the-ordinary that it was one of the few sentences recorded for posterity by His disciples. "It is more blessed to give than to receive." While He practiced it, the apostles questioned it, and the masses doubted it. Thus it was—and, we might add—is now, and ever more shall be. The discovery that there is joy in creative giving always comes as a fresh surprise.

Philanthropy began with individuals giving because of their love, concern, and compassion for other individuals. As these persons prospered, they shared with those less fortunate than themselves in terms of family, friends, and acquaintances. Their circle of concern enlarged as the world shrank, until today we have come to recognize that we all live in a global village.

As persons' awareness of needs increased, there came the realization that circumstances existed with which individuals simply could not cope by themselves—the widow, the orphan, the family whose home has just burned, the village destroyed by flood, the community shaken and shattered by an earthquake. As individuals found others with like concerns, they organized, pooled their resources, and shared in group causes. One person could perhaps help another; hundreds could help dozens; thousands could help hundreds; and millions could aid a whole area where persons suffer from a single catastrophe.

As such groups organized and expressed their concerns, they also defined the purposes of their benevolence. Some were concerned with food, clothing, and housing. Some were concerned with physical, mental, and social needs. Some were concerned with children, youth, and the aged. Some were concerned with the handicapped, retarded, and exceptional. Some were concerned with basic needs, improved standards of living, and the environment. Today, in every area of concern, there are literally dozens of groups addressing their humanitarian concerns and sharing their resources to resolve particular problems and ameliorate situations in the human-moral-spiritual realms.

Such complexity has created other complexities. As groups for giving grew larger and larger, they faced a need to become institutional. Professional staff, research, applied methodology, policy, and defined procedures became the order of the day. Government required incorporation to ensure registration, conformity to statute and code, and responsibility. This provided protection for appointed stewards of resources should they stumble into misjudgment or adverse circumstances. It also assured respect for the donor and the designated purpose of the donor's gift. Those individuals who abused privileges or failed to perform services consistent with the wishes of the giver were subject to criminal action. Institutions that failed to meet their responsibilities stood to lose their charters. For it was intended that these institutions or organizations be extensions of ourselves and form a part of our voluntary giving.

In the beginning, human society survived on a barter system. In time, this barter market was transformed into a cash market. Cash and carry were the watchwords, and everything had its price. If people had money, they bought. If they did not have money, they waited until adequate monetary resources were available or else went without the article in question.

With the development of banking, our cash-and-carry society became a check-writing society. Less time was required to pay obligations. Mail orders, telephone orders, and messenger services became the channels through which one was billed, and in time we would mail a check in payment for the commodities delivered.

The check-writing procedure paved the way for the deferred-payment plan. Each consumer was given a line of credit, with his borrowing or purchases of commodities on credit limited to that line of credit. Regular payments were required and these payments were governed in size by the amount of the obligation. Service charges or interest, as the case might be, were added based on the amount of indebtedness remaining from the preceding month or billing period. The deferred-payment procedure has required more than paper orders and check-writing activities. The route has been enhanced by credit cards, bank cards, and computer processes.

Now we are at the threshold of a new tomorrow. In the supermarket, coded commodities pass over electronic scanners, and price and inventory controls are computed. Consumers' personal bank accounts are debited as their bank cards are placed into the computer to transfer their funds to the retailers' accounts. Engineers and accountants presently are creating even more sophisticated procedures whereby funds are transferred from the consumer to the retailer, the wholesaler, and the distributor at the same instant. As we look to the road ahead, it is very possible that we may see a purchase of a quart of milk at the grocery store initiating, in domino fashion, a series of funds transfers—in a single instant—affecting the accounts of the distributor, the dairyman, and a feed supplier a thousand miles away.

These procedures are not confined to the market place. Increasingly, they are common to the home, the school, the church, the opera, the art gallery, and the museum.

As a clergyman, I have insisted that unless the church is "tuned in" to these new fiscal procedures it will be "tuned out." The results: penniless churches in a cashless society. And what I say of the church may be said of every charitable organization we identify in this twentieth-century society, from the Ladies' Aid Society to the American Red Cross, from the Brownie Scouts to the Boston Symphony Orchestra.

The climate has changed, and we are subject to these changes.

In philanthropy, we have moved from individual to group and institution. In support, we have moved from personal to delegated. In resources, we have moved from gift-in-kind to the coin of the realm, from the coin of the realm to the checkbook, from the checkbook to automatic funds transfer systems.

Philantrophy is dependent upon funding processes. The utilization of these processes makes personal participation possible. Only as we become attuned to these processes will we be capable of contributing to, and sharing in support of, humanitarian services.

For most of us, cash gifts are the easiest to handle. They make up the largest segment of our giving, and it would be impossible for one person to list the hundreds of organizations, clubs, chapters, societies, and associations that bid for our support.

Available statistics do not adequately reflect total giving in the local churches, in denominational causes, or through related agencies. The Sunday schools, women's associations, men's clubs, youth organizations, organized classes, interest groups, societies, and clubs supported by cash gifts and subscriptions, car washes and cake sales, square dances and excursions, and benefit movies and world tours compose a formidable but largely unreported portion of our national philantrophic portrait.

From earliest experiences in voluntary agencies and movements, we nurture individuals in the buying-for-benefit concept. Cub Scouts, Brownie Scouts, Boy Scouts, Girl Scouts, Boy's Clubs, Campfire Girls, Catholic Youth Organization, Young Men's Christian Association, Young Women's Christian Association, Young Men's Hebrew Association, Young Women's Hebrew Association, Junior League, Rotary, Kiwanis, Optimist, Lions, Sertoma, and senior citizens' clubs—all, from the cradle to the grave, gain a sizable portion of their financial resources for their programs from benefit sales that range from candy bars to doughnuts, from light bulbs to flares, and from "booster stickers" to "patron certificates."

Promoters are at work broadening the spectrum of purchase-for-benefit offerings, and the seemingly incidental gives way to major proportions. The Holy Year, pilgrimages to Palestine, European theater tours have all been developed to benefit churches, synagogues, organizations, and clubs, a portion of a travel agency's commission being shared with a charitable organization in sales incentive plans and arrangements.

The Disabled Veterans Organization mails a miniature of your automobile license plate, hoping that you will "buy" it to support activities among disabled veterans. An organization in Des Moines, Iowa, mails packets of greeting cards with the hope that you will "buy" them to assist in the group's services to the blind. An Appalachian Mountain Service Agency mails sheets of address labels anticipating your willingness to "buy" them to assist in their program.

Every time we think that the purchase-for-benefit approach surely has reached saturation, we are suddenly aware of new commodities available for the benefit of favorite charities. So extensive is the procedure that a visit to an undertaking parlor or a ride in a demonstration car may provide financial assistance to a child attending camp!

Buy! Try! These two pave an avenue of approach in voluntary giving.

For some, gifts-in-kind are more convenient. A local church has a rummage sale, and the items sold are largely things that have been contributed as gifts-in-kind. Early in my ministry, I served as an area director for the Christian Rural Overseas Program with responsibility in seven counties of western Illinois. This was a part-time position in connection with a small-town pastorate. Our endeavor was to solicit gifts of corn, soybeans, and wheat to feed hungry persons abroad. The effort was most successful where we could enlist the interest of a grain elevator manager, so that as farmers brought their grain to market the weighmaster would ask, "How much do you want to give to CROP?" Five bushels of corn here, ten bushels of wheat there, and twenty-five bushels of soybeans somewhere else added up to substantial quantities to meet needs among the world's impoverished.

Our system of philanthropy consists of a network of voluntary service. Twenty-one national agencies reported 84,000,000 volunteers in 1982, and this did not include over 3,500,000 persons who contributed blood through the American Red Cross Blood Bank or an additional 7,700,000 students who participated in Red Cross programs in our schools. Nor did it include those who participate in the organizational life of our churches, synagogues, schools, hospitals, lodges, clubs, or local service organizations. Total them, and it is difficult to find anyone anywhere who is not somehow involved in our system of philanthropy, either as a volunteer in service or soliciting support, or in the support itself.

Philanthropic bequests provide sizable sums also.

The exclusion on the estate of the first spouse expiring, and increases in the tax exclusion on estates that in 1987 will total $600,000, have reduced bequested income to nonprofit organizations substantially. Bequests in 1983, however, represented 7.0 percent of all philanthropic giving in the United States. This came to $4.52 billion. This is still an impressive sum!

What claims do various organizations have upon our lives? What obligation do we have to respond to their appeals? What portion of our livelihood can they rightfully expect or demand? What criteria may we use to determine priorities among them? What part of our living will we give to each group soliciting our resources and matching our priorities? These are important questions, and the answers are certainly not simple to come by. With substantial portions of our capability and resources on requisition, we, as individuals, must learn to respond intelligently and responsibly.

Organizations do this through the grant processes and program structures they have devised. Subject to the same influences as individuals, corporations and foundations have sought to retain the integrity and identity of the gift and the satisfaction that comes in effecting change through giving by establishing grants and grant processes programmed to make a difference. There are few corporations and foundations that respond to all askings, dividing their resources arbitrarily, and concluding that they have given something to everything in the hope that some good will come out of some of it. Instead, they have studied their options, selected causes, monitored services, and effected change! They have discovered the joy of sharing and the art of creative giving!

Two aspects are unique to corporate giving in today's society. First, corporations tend to confine their gifts geographically to the areas where they have manufacturing plants and distribution centers. Second, many corporations provide support through challenge gifts, which means they match the contributions of their employees to educational institutions and select causes. Charity choices build employee morale at one company. Prentice-Hall, the research and publishing concern, reports that one employer sets an annual contribution budget, then invites employees to name their favorite charities. Employees then are permitted to send the company's checks to the charities in their own names.

In Manila, during the month of March 1974, in a stop on an around-the-world tour, I visited a depot for the receiving and distribution of surplus and obsolete medical supplies donated by Western pharmaceutical and surgical supply houses. Everything from sutures to intravenous medication had been provided for the healing of underpriveleged persons in an underdeveloped nation.

Later, in still another area of the Philippines, Upi, high in the hills far distant from Cotabata, I saw agricultural equipment contributed by American manufacturers. And, in Orange, Pakistan, wells were being drilled with equipment contributed by American industry.

Corporate support is an unusual component in our philanthropic society because the contributions come from the employees and/or investors. Salaries and dividends would both be larger, we can assume, were it not for corporate philanthropy. When we feed into the mental computer such giving and the tax factor, however, the difference is very, very small.

Individuals unable or unwilling to cope with the established requirements for procedures in private foundations have moved their resources into community foundations. These foundations have had a remarkable growth over the past sixteen years. In community foundations, endowments are administered under the direction of a representative governing body responsible for charitable activities. Donors often specify, or designate, a purpose for their gifts at the time their funds are contributed to the community foundation. Or they may reserve the right of subsequent review. Inasmuch as community foundations qualify as "public charities," regulations applicable to private foundations do not apply, and the procedure proves to be especially attractive to the private sector since the Tax Reform Act of 1969. Community foundations number in excess of 275. Assets in current dollars reached over $47.5 billion in 1981. Their grants in 1981 totalled $3.7 billion.

Community foundations, by virtue of their charters, restrict their activities and contributions to particular regions, and those moving resources from the private into the public sector do so respecting these limitations.

Our story of philanthropy began with individuals responding to human needs, person to person, family to family, and community to community. Now we are in the global village, and problems have increased in size and enlarged in scope. Greater and greater resources are needed to effect solutions. The service organization and charitable institution are products of necessity as society continues to respond to basic human needs.

The dominant tendency has been to proceed from the personal to the impersonal. Direct support from donor to recipient has been replaced by donor support to charitable agency or institution. This development offers obvious advantages in efficiency, but it is difficult to gauge the importance of the gift and measure its effectiveness in this impersonal system.

The impersonal aspect is complicated by fiscal change and the development of computer processes programmed to transfer gifts automatically from cash or credit reserves to charitable agencies and institutions. In some cases, the benefits accruing to dependent individuals are also computer programmed. One county in New York State began the distribution of welfare benefits through electronic funds transfers to accounts of individual recipients on September 1, 1975. Between 1973 and 1985, the number of persons receiving Social Security benefits through Direct Deposit (an electronic funds transfer process) has increased from 4.7 million to 18.3 million. Forty percent of all Social Security recipients have now elected to receive payments through the electronic funds transfer process.

It is time for us as individuals to discover new models for creative giving that will respond to human needs, conform to statute limitations, and utilize fully the procedures and capabilities of these service institutions and organizations, so that they become truly the extension of ourselves in meeting human needs and bringing to fulfillment our innermost hopes and prayers for our fellow beings.

2

A Challenge
to Creative Giving

Jesus of Nazareth is quoted by His disciples as saying: "It is more blessed to give than to receive." While there are mature persons in almost every society around the world who are convinced of this, the principle does not seem to be inborn. Indeed, the reverse is apt to be the case! At least when I review my own childhood, I must admit I was firmly convinced for years that it was more blessed to receive than to give. Holidays and holy days were significant for what I could expect to receive, and my expectations always exceeded the buying potential of parents and relatives. Children's Day was always a problem to me. Mother received gifts on Mother's Day. Father received gifts on Father's Day. But on Children's Day there were no gifts. Usually, Children's Day observance was limited to the ritual of going to church, standing before the congregation, and reciting some verse or poem to the effect that it is great to be alive, childhood years are the best years, and parents and others would do well to be thankful that they have us children around.

In fact, the philanthropic dimension in life for most children is a slow discovery. But when it comes, it is a glorious experience. I recall that in his first year of school our oldest son had made a gift to be presented to his mother and me for Christmas. He was so excited about the gift that he could not keep it a secret, and so daily he talked about the Christmas present he was making for us in school. He let the cat out of the bag, in fact, by even telling us what it was. A presser! Our only problem was that we had no idea what

9

a presser was. Daily his enthusiasm for the gift increased, and that enthusiasm kept pace with our curiosity concerning this first gift from our oldest son. On Christmas Eve, it was our privilege to open the gift, and what do you suppose it was? A blotter! He carefully had designed a "presser" with whatever artistic talent he had, and it became for him a gift of love. Would that all our philanthropy could flower with such great enthusiasm and joy.

Try this exercise. Think back through the years, and see if you can discover that early event in your own experience when you made a first step forward, at least, in understanding that it is more blessed to give than to receive.

If you are like most of us, you will probably find that this understanding had its birth in the normal involvements of family and community life. Our discovery of the joy of giving almost never has its beginnings in abstract commitment. Almost certainly, you will find in your experience something similar to one of these:

- A neighbor's barn burns down. Not only did he suffer the loss of the building, but feed for his horses and cattle went up in smoke as well. Even his cows were destroyed. You, with neighbors, responded to human need. One gave a milk cow and another a calf. One gave a bale of hay and another a bushel of oats. One gave boards and another roofing paper. The neighbors had a barn-raising, and because folk cared enough to share their best, the family soon was well on the way to economic recovery.

- A relative was seriously injured in an automobile accident caused by a hit-and-run driver, and personal insurance was not adequate to cover the loss. Family members came to the rescue to help the victim meet medical bills, provide adequate care during the period of recovery, and give sufficient financial assistance to enable the person to purchase another car to provide for transportation to and from work.

- A church burned. It had been the gathering place for folk from all around. Indeed, if there was a recreation center in the community, it was the church. Sundays, weekends, after school, and on holidays, local life revolved around the programs put on there. A merchant provided the use of a garage, the theater owner opened the doors of his theater for Sunday morning religious services, friends and neighbors provided free-will offerings and gifts-in-kind. The programs continued almost without interruption because each person did his or her part.

These illustrations are from real life, and in one degree or another they are almost certainly close to your personal experience. They provide a basis for our understanding of what philanthropy is all about and of the process by which we, as children and young adults, become involved.

Gradually, however, our philanthropy loses the magic of relating to persons. Under the pressures of social complexity, it recedes into the impersonal. A Girl Scout comes to your door and invites you to buy a box of Girl Scout cookies. They do not represent the best buy in the world, and they may not be the best cookies under the sun. But you buy. Why? *First,* because the girl is engaged in an unselfish enterprise. She is doing the work and getting few of the benefits or resources. There is no commission for her. Does she get points? Perhaps. But the profits go to the Girl Scout organization and the concerns its members share. *Second,* you buy because you want to be a part of these concerns and interests. You want to encourage the girl. You want to support the organization. You want a better society tomorrow.

Much of our philanthropy has moved away from giving in direct personal response to particular needs and situations and instead involves organizational and institutional structures. One could list literally thousands that provide opportunities to support programs, advance causes, render services, expand horizons, and meet human needs.

A man in the City of Brotherly Love confided to me that he was contributing to 178 organizations and agencies in Philadelphia, Pennsylvania, and across the United States. The total of his support was impressive. Yet none of it was really making an impact on society or accomplishing what he most wanted his personal philanthropy to do. Isn't this true of most of us? Over many years, we make contributions by check and annually identify and list them with our tax return. A dollar here, $2 there, and $25 somewhere else come to a sizable sum when all are added together. But individually, many hardly make a difference. The truth is, some of these contributions prove to be liabilities instead of assets to the organizations receiving them. Processing costs absorb more than the value of the gift. But there they are—a pattern from the past that will project far into the future.

I said to may friend in Philadelphia: "Suppose you were to go over the list and select perhaps twenty-five? Suppose among the twenty-five you were to select five for primary support and change? Which would you select?" He was startled by the challenge and enthused over the prospect of "meaningful philanthropy" that opened up when he responded to it, exclaiming, "All these years I've just been giving my money away. Now I can really do something!"

At that point in his life, there were two things that he needed to do. *First*, he needed to make a realistic analysis of his giving potential both short term and long term. *Second*, he needed to define his objectives in philanthropy. These two deserve to be considered in greater detail.

A realistic analysis of giving potential. Ordinarily, we would assume that his giving potential would be closely related to what is being given. It may be. Then, again it may not. It is quite likely that potential exceeds performance. My friend itemized his giving to the 178 organizations or agencies to which he contributed. Put those to the test of the adding machine, and you will arrive at a figure of giving support based on past experience. The individual gifts varied in size. Some amounted to hundreds of dollars and some to single dollars; some were in twenty-five-dollar and others in ten- and five-dollar denominations. The total? A sizable sum of money. But few or none of these several dozen contributions were made as the result of real enthusiasm for a particular cause.

Because his giving was too much a matter of response and not enough a matter of purpose, there was not a great deal of rhyme or reason in his giving. He could not explain why some charities figured more significantly in dollar amounts than others. Gradually, however, we discovered keys: *a)* personal contacts had elicited some support, *b)* memberships in church, lodge, and other organizations were responsible for larger gifts, and *c)* annual or quarterly appeals received in the mail got a routine response of a dollar or two each.

Much to our mutual surprise, his giving was not a matter of budget. It related to "cash flow" and "loose money" in his checking account. When appeals accumulated in his desk drawer to the extent that he thought he should do something about them, he began writing and mailing checks. When the checkbook balance had reached the limit of his generosity, the ritual terminated until the volume of unattended matters in his desk drawer called for attention again and checkbook balances permitted consideration.

Through the years, his financial support of causes and charities increased. This was not so much because his income had increased or because the appeals from organizations benefiting from his generosity were more direct and appealing, but primarily because the number of appeals had increased. Certain charities had learned of his generosity to one charity and through exchange or purchase of lists had gained a new prospect, and he had responded regularly and well.

But when his support of charitable organizations and institutions was measured against his actual income, the story was not nearly as impressive as the list of 178 charities to which he contributed. In terms of actual worth, he was giving little; yet he considered himself generous and unselfish because 178 institutions and causes were in the picture of his concern. He, like many in our society, assumed that he was giving much because he was giving often.

He approached his accountant and financial adviser and discovered that he could increase his giving to charitable causes by 500 percent and that a sizable portion of this increase would be borne by the government under the Internal Revenue Code. While it would cost him a little over twice as much as he was previously giving out of his "living," so to speak, in real dollars he would actually be distributing five times as much. His giving had averaged $2,000 a year. His giving potential, reasonably assessed by a qualified accountant, was $10,000 a year. The resulting reduction in taxable income would pick up almost half of it.

Having discovered this, he next had to define some objectives. What did he really want to do with his money? Which were the deserving causes for which he could make a difference? How could he program his giving to get the greatest mileage from his dollars?

He did not feel that he could make a decision without first exploring the several areas of concern to which folk contribute their charitable dollars. He was looking for areas of need and percentages of response. Here is what he found:

TABLE 1. DISTRIBUTION OF CHARITABLE DOLLARS, 1983

Causes	Percentages
Religion	47.8
Health and Hospitals	14.1
Education	13.9
Social Welfare	10.7
Arts and Humanities	6.3
Civic and Public	2.8
Other	4.4

Source: Giving USA, 1984 Annual Report, American Association of Fund-Raising Counsel, Inc.

Against these, it was time for him to define objectives. What were his lifetime priorities? Which were the areas of his greatest concern? In surveying the human situation, how could he lessen the hurt and bring hope to the future?

As he looked to his resources, he discovered that they represented two lives: a life of earning and a life of spending; a life of receiving and a life of giving. In gainful employment, he exercised his talents where they could make the greatest difference, increase his earning power, and expand his resources. Except in the area of his investments he had not thought in those terms when it came to distributing what he had gained. Charitable giving was furthest from his mind.

He needed to take a careful look at causes, his giving potential that had now become a commitment, and a projection as to what he could hope to accomplish through his share in charitable giving. Because he was a man still in life's prime, he needed to consider not only a single year of giving but giving over the long haul; not $10,000 in one year but $100,000 or more over ten years. This required the setting of goals—goals for the present, the short term, and the long term. At this moment, he discovered life at a most interesting threshold of human experience.

In the course of this examination of giving, my Philadelphia friend made some interesting discoveries about the ways in which people give. Religion seemed to be getting the top dollar. *The Year-*

book of American and Canadian Churches 1984 reported that forty
U.S. communions, with a full or confirmed membership of 41,618,179
persons, received $10,902,028,177. This equaled per capita giving
of $261.95. Of this amount, 80.73 percent went toward individual
congregational expenses and 19.27 percent for benevolences.

At the top of the list among the forty religious bodies, or denominations, he found the Missionary Church, Inc., with per capita
giving of $844.46. Much to his surprise, he discovered members of
his own church, The United Methodist Church, near the bottom of
the list—$189.78. He wondered why. He discovered that while
members of the Missionary Church tithe, practically all of their
giving is through congregational and denominational channels;
however, members of his own church and the so-called main-line
denominations approach Christian mission both through the
church and through the community. Total giving is not confined
to, nor does it stop at, the local church or particular denomination.

Members of his United Methodist Church—in common with
those of most of the main-line denominations—were less generous
in giving to their local church and denomination. But, because
their giving was by no means limited to these channels, they were
not necessarily less generous as philanthropists when their charitable contributions to colleges and universities, hospitals and institutions, and civic and public enterprises needing support were taken
into account. In light of all this information he had to determine
whether religious organizations and institutions would challenge
him to a 47.8 percent volume in dollar support or whether the
interests and concerns in the arts and humanities would challenge
him to respond with greater support than the 6.3 percent of
charitable dollars contributed in 1983.

The experience of my Philadelphia friend is by no means unique.
We can all profit from such an examination of our own giving, as
well as giving patterns in general. Our potential for giving is great.
Present tax structures encourage personal philanthropy. We are
challenged to discover new models for creative giving. We are
challenged to utilize these new models to the greatest extent as we
discover again the joy of giving.

True, my friend was a moderately wealthy man, and the dollar
amounts of his contributions are impressive. But the same exercise
is equally useful for all of us. Suppose a person with an adjusted

gross income of $10,000 were to distribute $572 among 178 causes; he would not accomplish much. But if one were to give $200 to one, $100 each to two others, and $75 each to three others, the contributions would be significant.

In 1982, itemized contributions from individuals ranged from 1.75 to 14.85 percent of adjusted gross income. Actual average percentages in comparison to adjusted gross income were as follows:

TABLE 2. CONTRIBUTIONS BY ADJUSTED GROSS INCOME, 1982

Category	Average contributed	Percentage of income
Under $10,000	$572	5.72%
$10,000 to $15,000	$671	4.47%
$15,000 to $30,000	$725	2.42%
$30,000 to $50,000	$948	1.90%
$50,000 to $100,000	$1,751	1.75%
$100,000 to $200,000	$4,578	2.29%
$200,000 to $500,000	$12,199	2.44%
$500,000 to $1,000,000	$36,435	3.64%
$1,000,000 & over	$148,543	14.85%

Compiled from Internal Revenue Service statistics.

We give much! We have much to give! We can do much through personal philanthropy!

This book is addressed to those of you who give $572 a year, and it is addressed to those who give $148,543 a year. It is addressed to those who are basically responsible for the bulk of our charitable contributions and who yet have not discovered the joy of sharing.

The recovery of the joy of giving, a joy as elementary as that of a first-grade child making a presser and presenting it to his parents as his first Christmas gift, requires that we make a listing of our majors and minors, the large and the small, and those intended to make a difference. Having done so, we are ready to face the real challenge to creative giving.

3

Selecting Causes and Structuring Priorities

I visited a service center in Surabaya, Indonesia, in 1974. The center was located in an area where family incomes averaged only $12 a month, and there is an average of eight children in every family. The center was related to nonprofit agencies in the United States, some of which contract for services to dependent people. Through one such agency, donors in the United States could elect to support a child in Indonesia for $15 a month. The agency would make funds available to the center, donors would be paired with donees, and letters exchanged periodically. I inquired of my host: "How much does each child receive of the fifteen dollars contributed for his benefit in the United States?" His answer: "Six dollars and fifty cents." I thought how wonderful it was that folk were sharing so generously to augment family incomes in Indonesia so substantially and expressed my gratitude to my host as we viewed children copying letters to be sent to benefactors thousands of miles away. He responded: "But if these gifts were to be channeled through Church World Service, we would receive here in Surabaya fourteen dollars and fifty-five cents of each fifteen dollars contributed!"

Such an incident illustrates the problems and opportunities to be faced when we seek creativity in our giving. In this case, the cause was alleviating hunger. And in the United States, large numbers of people had selected this cause as one to which they would contribute. Some chose to send their gifts through their church. Because the major denominations have established an ecumenical agency to work with this problem around the world, giving in this way meant, for example, that Methodist gifts might eventually accomplish their purpose through an Episcopal mission in Indonesia. Through this channel, 97 cents of every dollar could be used directly in relief measures. To achieve this efficiency, however, donors could be permitted to choose only the area of the world in which they wished their money used; they could not be more specific than that. Donors who wanted to be provided with the name of the particular child or family to be helped and who chose to develop a personal relationship between themselves and the donees through an exchange of pictures and correspondence were forced to contribute through some other channel. While specific, this alternate route was expensive—57 percent of their gift was absorbed in administrative costs.

Perhaps donors had not realized that there could be a difference. Perhaps all assumed that a gift given is a gift received. Had some realized that they could designate a gift, and in exchange receive some acknowledgments and pictures, perhaps they would have gone the child-sponsor route. Some going the sponsor route might have selected denominational-ecumenical channels had they known that 97 percent of their gift could go directly to relieve human need and suffering, although the personal touch would have been lacking. It may be that few could provide a reason for the course they chose to follow.

Selecting causes and structuring priorities is important. The process tends to revolve around such questions as: How many people do we want to help? How much grain do we want to provide? What volume of medical and clinical services do we wish to ensure? What educational opportunities do we want to give? What is the cost of the delivery of services and commodities? How much of our gift is absorbed in soliciting our support?

Five factors should figure in personal philanthropy as one selects causes and structures priorities.

First, there is the economic factor. Every gift has an economic impact of some kind, and this impact must be traced if the true significance of the gift is to be understood. This factor was certainly at work in Indonesia, as we have already seen. But the economic factor in our giving is more subtle still.

Indonesia is a developing nation—more developed than some, less developed than others. Increasingly, it is becoming a major influence in the world's economy and in world markets. Natural resources from Indonesia are important. The development of those resources is increasingly important. But the way in which financial assistance is provided through philanthropy will determine how mature that nation becomes in the community of nations and how independent its people will be, not only in developing their resources but also in determining what influence those resources will have on the world today and the world's peoples tomorrow. One philanthropic strategy, for example, will provide assistance to unskilled and uneducated people that will enable them to play a major role in their emerging technological society. Another strategy might enable these same persons to become more productive, while withholding from them the training that would permit them to manage the development of their resources according to the value systems of their particular society.

Economic factors come into play in our philanthropic giving as we think of where we are willing to have our gifts used. In Western civilization, we consider ourselves a part of the free world with an open economy. Some donors are determined that their funds shall be used only in areas that provide their peoples with these same privileges of free enterprise, open competition, and self-determination. Some donors, on the other hand, believe in the principle of self-determination so completely that they will make donations even in a closed society on the assumption that people must have the freedom to select whatever social structures they deem best suited to their human needs. Some donors will say: "If they are free, we will give. If they are not free, we will not give." Other donors will say: "If this is the course they choose, this is all right with me. I want to help regardless of the economic system."

Economic factors are also at work in determining the costs of the philanthropic process itself. In Indonesia, I praised an effort that provided a specific family with $6.50 out of each $15.00 donated to the cause. Another observer might question the wisdom of so restricted a gift, especially because funds could be channeled to the same area through programs that operated with greater freedom at much less cost—providing, in fact, $14.55 out of each $15.00.

There is a danger, however, that as expenses rise and governments demand greater efficiency and economy in philanthropic organizations, we may place too great an emphasis on administrative costs. A national network documentary on philanthropic organizations and giving was presented in December 1975 in which the high cost of administering our gifts was severely criticized. The salaries for administrators, as high as $50,000 a year, were questioned. Administrative costs for international organizations were deplored, coming as high as 87 percent of gifts in certain situations. Fund-development procedures carried out under the banner of religion, which were actually little more than rip-offs, were severely criticized.

Of the factors brought into focus, the salary issue was not the most alarming to me, for when philanthropy manages billions of dollars a year in cash and commodities, it is reasonable that administrators with qualifications and expertise be obtained to guide such efforts. However, when gifts do little more than support the organization processing them, there is no justification for their existence in the long term, and individuals, through their giving, must determine whether or not those types of institutions and organizations survive.

Some mention, finally, deserves to be made of the economic factor and our motives for giving. Early Christians gave all that they had. Everything they had was held in common. Each received according to his or her needs. Today, far too many of us tend to give out of convenience, little realizing that our capacity to give is great and that an incentive to give is built into the Internal Revenue Code.

We are a free society dedicated to providing services through voluntary organizations. We have a lot to give! Through giving, we can make a difference!

Second, there is the social factor. This same project in Indonesia provided an ironic instance. In the course of my visit, I asked, "How are families selected to take part in this program?" "On the basis of need," was the reply. "Usually, families where there is no father to provide for them are given special consideration. Unfortunately, one of our problems now is that fathers are leaving their families to make their wives and children eligible for this kind of designated support. Even though only six dollars and fifty cents of each fifteen-dollar gift eventually reaches the needy family, even that sum is more than a man can earn!" A failure to recognize the social significance of the philanthropy, or to respond to it in time, was creating a devastating social problem fully as significant as the situation the program had originally been intended to correct.

But even this was not the end. In one case, the donors had sought to foster self-determination and independence in the recipients by providing them with a cash allowance. A family is free to determine what it considers to be its basic needs and what course it will take to meet those needs through decisions in the marketplace. In these situations, the family is independent. The degree of independence may be illusory, however, because accounting procedures and the requirement of a quarterly letter may tend to undermine the full discretion we assume.

On the other hand, when gift processes provide commodities and services, the social impact is quite different. The recipients are kept more closely tied to the agency and tend to identify themselves more completely with others benefiting from the program. Those dispensing the gifts become the parents. Those receiving the gifts become the children. In some situations, they must identify with organized religion, while others will insist that there can be no religious identification at all. In each case, there is a social impact related to the gift. In the Indonesian situation, as a matter of fact, the one agency provided an umbrella under which both religious and secular organizations functioned. The administrator served an ecumenical agency and contracted with other agencies for particular resources to meet specific human needs. The building itself was arranged in such a way that the religious relationships were evident in certain areas, and the secular was in complete control of others. Both areas had social implications; yet donors frequently chose certain courses for their philanthropic dollars to take without any real understanding of the implications.

Human rights, equal rights, and freedom of religion will be important factors in selecting causes and structuring priorities through philanthropic giving.

Third, there is the religious factor. Much of our philanthropy finds its origin in religious institutions and religious life. This is especially true here in the United States, where many of our organizations are church related, or at least have their origin in denominational structures.

In my travels in all fifty states, I have been amazed at the great number of people, especially in business, who say that they will not contribute anything to religion or to philanthropic organizations that they assume to be religious. And many of our philanthropic organizations, seeking to capture this kind of support, have cut loose from any relationship whatever to organized religion. But I have yet to see a philanthropic organization that is not religious. It may not be Christian. It may not be denominational. It may not be Roman Catholic, Protestant, Orthodox, or Jewish. But, believe me, it is religious. Ethical and moral judgments governing philosopical outlook and administrative policies are certainly religious in their rootage, and no philanthropy of which I am aware operates without making such judgment on a daily basis.

In selecting causes and structuring priorities, religious concerns are of great importance to many in both the religious and secular worlds. Every gift we make has evangelistic implications! What gospel will we proclaim? Is it the Christian gospel? Is it the secular gospel? Is it a sectarian gospel? Is it an ecumenical gospel? Is it an atheistic or agnostic gospel?

The religious factor was at work in the Indonesian program we have been using as an illustration throughout this chapter. One funding procedure frankly labeled itself "Christian," although it was related to no ecclesiastical structure. The other funding procedure was denominational in its origin, although it was administered ecumenically. The one termed "Christian" was not ecclesiastically oriented or structured. The other was of "Christian" origin, but not so labeled.

Many people insist that their religious faith be evident in any program designated to meet human needs, if the program is to have their support. It may be a Baptist making a gift to a Baptist church to assist a Baptist mission to convert nationals to the Baptist faith through development. In Orange, Pakistan, I met a tourist who was terribly distressed because the name of his particular denomination was not stamped on the bags of grain being distributed to Bengali refugees. As we ate together in a hotel dining room, he confided to me that if he had known the true situation he would not have given! Yet if the symbol of his denomination had been on the container, someone from another denomination might not have given. Certainly, there are some who would not give if any religious identification at all were evident.

At the same time, religion also must be recognized as a most powerful motivating factor in our giving. The Parenthood of God and the family of persons require reasonable and responsible concern for others in modern society. Every generation has answered Cain's question, "Am I my brother's keeper?" with a single response: "You are!" We are, also! Whether one is black, white, yellow, red, or brown; young or old; rich or poor; strong or weak; female or male—we are at times dependent upon others and always responsible for others.

Humans are religious creatures, and the greater the spiritual commitment, the more generous the response to meeting basic human needs for others. For most, the concept of God requires it. Implanted deep in the religious human consciousness are the words: "Inasmuch as ye have done it unto one of the least of these, my brethren, ye have done it unto me."

We will select causes and structure priorities in terms of our religious convictions and those aspects of religion we deem important in this believing world.

Fourth, there is a political factor. Political forces are at work as never before as Western civilization becomes a minority influence in denominational and national political structures. Our philanthropy has political implications.

One need not go far from home in this world to become conscious of one's presence as an "ugly American." This situation has had a profound impact on the missionary movement. Many Christians have been unfairly critical of their denominational administrators and the fact that most denominations have far fewer missionaries abroad than in any other period of our modern history. There are two reasons for this: nationals have been educated and trained to be as fully qualified as those previously sent out by mission boards; and nationals can communicate while foreigners are no longer acceptable in most cultures. Hence, denominations have reduced mission staff and in the foreign mission field are developing strategy with nationals with far greater success than they otherwise could have.

On the broader scene, many people insist that their political presence be felt through the gift they give. Many insist that Uncle Sam be clearly identified on every parcel crossing international waters and that those who receive the supplies know that this is what Uncle Sam is doing for them. Because so much of our initiative has taken this course, much of the good we have done, and would do, is interpreted as Western imperialism.

But the political factor is not limited to nationhood. There are many kinds of groups whose members insist on identification. Because they represent pressure groups of one kind or another, they deserve to be classified as essentially political in character. There are some who insist on the identification of their race; some, on the identification of their sex! There are some who make certain that their contributions will be channeled through the Women's First National Bank of New York to women in Indonesia and that the parcels will be identified as being contributed from women in New York City to women in Surabaya, Indonesia.

The political factor, broadly considered, influences the ways in which we respond to appeals. Many organizations make their appeals on the basis of names available as sponsors. There is a tendency to assume that when a persons' name appears on an organization's stationery, the person of influence has carefully investigated the organization and attests to the legitimacy and credibility of the organization. But it is sadly true that in offices, reception rooms, and residences across the country there are citations, plaques, and trophies that have been awarded by institutions and organizations to persons whose sole decision for lending the support of their names has been the very decoration, tribute, or award they knew they would receive as a so-called benefactor.

In the field of religion, the proud possessor of one name known by almost every person on the continent with at least a grammar school education acknowledges openly that his contribution to charitable organizations is restricted to the use of his name. The causes endorsed are determined by two factors! *One*, the approach, namely, how and by whom is the invitation extended? *Two*, what tribute is provided in exchange for the use of his name? The name is one coveted by many large national organizations, but the endorsement says nothing about the credibility, efficiency, and effectiveness of the organizations!

Fifth, there is the personal aspect of giving. In our illustration from Indonesia, we saw those who wanted personal identification in terms of both the donor and donee. The donor must be identified. The donee must be seen. So a picture of a Caucasian donor hangs in a simple hut in Indonesia, and a native says: "This is my American mother." Another picture sits on a dresser in a bedroom in the United States of a donee in simple Indonesian costume, and another native says: "This is my Indonesian son."

We give a lot. We have much to give. But little or nothing is given unless it provides satisfaction to the donor. There must be personal pleasure in giving. A little old woman with modest means in a pocket of poverty described it best when she said, "I like to give because it makes me feel good all over."

Such pleasure finally depends, of course, upon economic, social, religious, and political factors and the personal delight we may derive from the extension of ourselves through them. It is a selfish thing to say, perhaps, but nevertheless it is true: We give because it pleases us to do so!

Jesus affirmed that the Kingdom of God is here, now! Actually, we can all have a part of a "little bit of heaven" by sharing lives and resources for the common good. Our communities can be improved. We can meet the needs of people. Moral fibers can be strengthened. The crippled can be helped to walk, the blind to see, and the poorest to gain hope for tomorrow.

In selecting causes to which we will contribute and in structuring our priorities for giving, we will be influenced toward support or away from support by the economic, social, religious, political, and personal factors that are inescapable. One simply cannot avoid or disregard them. Through them, we will discover even greater pleasure in our giving. In fact, we will find joy through giving!

4

The Foundation Concept
in Budget Building

Name a foundation. It may have a billion dollars in assets. Its annual distribution through grants may add up to an impressive total, although this probably represents a modest 5 or 6 percent of its total worth. Now, consider your own capital worth. Look at your annual income. Add up the total of your giving over the past twelve months. If you are even average in your distribution of charitable dollars, you are probably giving a larger percent of your worth and income than many of the large foundations.

You give. Proportionately, you tend to give generously. You should not allow the difference in actual dollars to obscure the important lessons in gift-giving procedures that you can learn from the ways in which foundations operate.

Consider the Juliette M. Atherton Trust. (now incorporated in the Atherton Family Foundation).

The trust was established on December 21, 1915, when Juliette M. Atherton, widow of J. B. Atherton, transferred 1,500 shares of stock in J. B. Atherton Estate, Limited, to three of her children in trust as a means of continuing the support of charitable work she had maintained throughout her life. Charles H. Atherton, Mary A. Richards, and Frank C. Atherton served as the first trustees.

Before she died in 1921, Mrs. Atherton amended her trust so as to give up her originally retained rights to amend or revoke it. She gave up these rights in recognition of the faithful and efficient service performed by her trustees and in the faith that her purposes would be perpetuated by them and their successors.

The deed of the trust directs that the income from the trust fund is to be used for ". . . grants, loans, and other forms of payment toward assisting in the establishment, maintenance, or promotion of such religious, charitable, educational, benevolent, scientific, or other like purposes, works, or enterprises, whether public or private, including churches, societies, schools, colleges, hospitals, asylums, homes and like institutions and objects for the public benefit and including also the support and education of individuals during their attendance at any educational institutions, and whether to corporations, associations, or other organizations of any private individual or individuals, as the Trustees shall in each case in their discretion and of their own volition approve."

A fundamental policy of the trust is to concern itself primarily with projects in the State of Hawaii.

The trust contributes to worthy projects through tax-qualified organizations, established under sound principles for nonprofit organizations. It does not operate any institutions, nor does it conduct any projects directly.

In accordance with the intent of Juliette M. Atherton, founder of the trust, grants are made to religious programs of various Christian denominations. Grants are also made for special projects as well as for operating budgets and annual fund campaigns for physical plants, equipment, and general endowments of such organizations.

The trustees, who serve without compensation, ordinarily meet every other month to conduct the regular business of the trust, to pass upon investment matters, and to consider requests for grants and scholarships.

The trust distributed a total of $885,275 to tax-qualified organizations during 1974, the majority of which were located in the State of Hawaii. It awarded 164 grants and made 3 pledge commitments to be paid out of future income.

Education is a primary concern of the trustees. Slightly more than half the income distributed went to organizations and institutions educating children, youth, and adults.

Eight independent secondary schools located in Hawaii received contributions in support of building construction debt retirement. Appeals for financial assistance from organizations engaged in less traditional educational programs were most carefully considered by the trustees, as these requests reflected changing conditions in the community that called for new approaches in programming and increased flexibility in our educational institutions. Grants were awarded to support experimental alternative education programs, summer tutoring projects, teacher training workshops, the training of volunteers to work with deaf and blind children in an educational setting, and for adult education purposes. Grants were made to support special education activities, including programs for youngsters with speech problems or learning difficulties and for the mentally retarded. The trustees continued to encourage the expansion of perschool education with their support of three organizations operating day-care programs for very young children.

Within the broad category of social welfare, the trustees considered numerous proposals from organizations seeking funds to provide services to needy groups of people, both those troubled and those in trouble, whose various stressful situations and difficult life experiences called for organized helping efforts from the voluntary agencies of Hawaii. Grants were awarded for the purpose of assisting the emotionally ill, the dependent or poor elderly, low-income families with health needs, men and women on parole and probation, youth in isolated rural communities, recovered alcoholics in need of housing and employment, children in group homes and sheltered placements, the physically handicapped, and immigrant families. Several neighborhood organizations were aided in their organizing efforts toward greater self-help and involvement in community concerns. The trustees cooperated with the Aloha United Way and the State of Hawaii's Department of Social Services and Housing to ensure that low-income families were provided with appropriate social services by voluntary agencies. Contributions from the trust, designated as local matching funds, went to both the Department of Social Services and Housing Trust Fund and Aloha United Way to be used to obtain federal funds in the ratio of $1 from Hawaii for $3 of federal monies.

In determining the distribution of income among various organizations requesting financial aid, the trustees endeavored to carry out the intent of Juliette M. Atherton, founder of the trust, which, as expressed in the original Trust Indenture, directed that where reasonable to do so "aid and assistance to institutions and objects fostering the advancement and promotion of the principles of the Protestant-Christian religion and Christian charity, education and benevolences" should be considered. Fourteen religious organizations and churches were given partial support for church restoration, missionary activities, religious education, or youth work, and two churches were helped to purchase or repair pipe organs.

The trustees did not overlook the needs of organizations that enrich the community with their cultural and artistic offerings. Grants were awarded to twelve music, drama, and opera groups for support of their programs and to four museums to assist them in the preservation of objects of historical and cultural interest. The Iolani Palace restoration and refurbishing project was one. A grant from the trust enabled the Friends of Iolani Palace to employ a museum director to begin planning for the day when the palace can again be open to both residents and visitors.

The story of the Juliette M. Atherton Trust is an impressive story indeed. There are probably few who read it who do not say: "I wish that I could do something like that, too!" Actually, you can! Perhaps the number of grants will not be so great or the sums of money in grants so large. But the real significance of a well-run foundation lies in the way it gives as much as in the amount of money it gives. And each of us, in our own dimension of philanthropy, can learn from the foundation concept of giving and enjoy the privileges and satisfaction it affords.

What were the significant steps in the development of that trust? Actually, there were six:

- The provision of funds for philanthropic support. Juliette M. Atherton transferred 1,500 shares of stock of J. B. Atherton Estate, Limited, to three of her children in trust as a means of continuing the support of charitable work previously maintained by her throughout her life.
- The establishment of guidelines for the distribution of those resources. The funds of the trust were not to be scattered indiscriminately across the philanthropic field. This was focused giving.
- The development of a schedule for grants. Mrs. Atherton provided that the trustees would meet bimonthly to conduct the regular business of the trust, pass on investment matters, and consider requests for grants and scholarships.
- An evaluation of appeals and a determination of short-term

directions for primary interest. Primary interests through 164 grants and 3 pledge commitments in 1974 focused on education, with special concern for new approaches and increased flexibility in educational institutions; on welfare, with special concern that those ranging from the emotionally ill to recovered alcoholics be aided in organizing efforts toward greater self-help and involvement in community concerns; on religion, to provide aid and assistance to institutions and objects fostering the advancement and promotion of the principles of the Christian religion and Christian charity.

• The provision of support for projects in such ways as to generate additional support from other sources for further development. Contributions were made for the restoration and refurbishing of the Iolani Palace, challenging support from the State of Hawaii and the Friends of Iolani Palace, and grants were made as local matching funds to obtain federal monies for Hawaii on a three-to-one ratio—for each dollar provided, the federal government would give them three dollars more.

• A monitoring of grants and project needs. Pledge commitments were made for the future for efforts challenging sustained support as other project support would be terminated, either because the task was completed or because the institution or agency simply could not carry out the mandates of the project as outlined by the development officers.

Suppose that as an individual, or as a family, you follow this procedure in personal philanthropy.

First, provide the funds to support your philanthropic services. You can do this simply by establishing a special bank account through which all charitable contributions will be made.

To begin the account, you may choose to take a proportion of your savings. One person took 5 percent from a savings account to begin such a process. Or you may choose to open the account with the amount to be taken from a first month's income and earmarked for charitable contributions. Consistent and regular funding from income and/or earnings is important, and you may decide to take a percentage of both income and earnings each month and place it in the charitable contributions account, which, in a sense, is your very own foundation.

The short form for reporting income to the Department of Internal Revenue assumes automatically that 15 percent will have been given to charity. Few, I am sure, do so well. It may be that you will want to establish such a percentage for your personal philanthropy. Or you may select another amount either larger or smaller. Some will want to give 50 percent of their incomes, some 25 percent of their incomes.

The ancient Hebrews developed the concept of the tithe, meaning that one-tenth of what they produced or acquired was presented in the name of God through offerings that contributed not only to the solvency of the religious institution but also to the needs of the distressed. The principle has continued through the Judeo-Christian traditions and is often proclaimed, and sometimes required, by denominations in both traditions on this continent and around the world today.

Our model for creative giving does not require or limit itself to a tithe. The sums designated for contributions will vary from one situation to another, from one family to another, and from one time of life to another. Certainly, folk in many economic situations should be generous, and those with great financial resources should be most generous. As we discovered earlier in this book, however, the most generous generally are those of modest means; the most generous are among those with limited financial potential.

Our model for creative giving, therefore, does provide that a significant portion of one's resources be set aside as a share in American and world philanthropy. The foundation concept in budget-building requires that funding be reasonable in size and the funding view intelligent in scope—that is, not sporadic, unplanned, or ill-advised.

Authorization may be given to have the amount designated for charitable contributions automatically transferred from your regular bank account to the special account for personal philanthropy. It is important that the procedure be systematic and regular so that maximum resources may be available to enhance joy through giving.

Second, establish the guidelines for the distribution of your charitable contributions. What causes will you support? What agencies will you endorse? What needs will you endeavor to meet? What contributions will you make? Must the causes you support be religious or secular? Must the causes you support meet human needs directly or contribute to research to alleviate human suffering? Will you provide for the needs of children, youth, adults, or the aged? Will you provide for the needs of particular racial or ethnic groups? Will you support efforts that meet human needs only in your neighborhood, your state, your nation, or particular nations?

Few have considered such questions before. But as we have noted, if you will look over your charitable contributions in past years, you will probably find a design emerging that reflects your interests and priorities.

How much did you give? Which were the large gifts? Which were the small gifts? Which gifts actually provided program- and service-funding for the charitable organization? Which gifts were actually a burden to the organization in its accounting processes—processes that seem insignificant to us as individuals but are supremely important to the organization if it is to function in the corporate structure of these times? In considering these questions, you must realize that a contribution of $14.69 or less is no gift at all. A gift of $2 may well cost an organization that amount, and $12.69 more, just to handle the contribution.

Having identified those gifts providing program funds and the delivery of services, those that were a definite liability to the organization, and those that we would consider marginal—perhaps a little in between—we need to consider our values. What do we deem important? What services do we want to provide? What do we really want our money to buy? How can we accomplish the greatest good with resources eternally modest when measured against seemingly infinite needs at home and abroad and universal in the global village?

With these questions in mind, we can begin a process of charitable budget-building. We have itemized our gifts during a fiscal year. We have defined those that constitute major support, minor support, and marginal support in terms of programming potential beyond the cost of developing and processing the individual gift.

Which gifts are important? Which gifts provide services that we can measure, that are significant, and that make a difference? Which gifts actually become an extension of self in accomplishing what we most want to do in this century of progress? We should provide for those causes generously. Others we may well eliminate until such time as their purposes and our priorities meet.

Third, develop a schedule for making grants. You will want to determine when grants will be made from your private "foundation." In the early stages, particularly, you may be tempted to write checks from this account as funds are available. With limited resources, it is probably wiser to wait several months before you begin making grants. If funds are left to accumulate over a period of time, the potential for sizable gifts increases and significant grants may be made to deserving causes as primary concerns come into focus. Monthly and bimonthly procedures are too frequent for most. Many choose to make grants three or four times a year. It is important that final grants be made before the closing of the fiscal year in order that you may take full advantage of your charitable contributions in filing your annual tax return.

You should remember that merely moving funds from one bank account to another does not constitute a qualified charitable contribution. The contribution becomes a qualified gift as it moves from your personal account to an organizational or institutional account. You should also remember that interest from funds in your personal contribution account, if a savings account, is earned and taxable income even when earmarked for charitable purposes.

At some point, consideration should be given to making at least some of these contributions on a programmed basis. There is nothing irrevocable about the processes. Even this procedure should be subject to periodic review and, of course, it is always possible to alter or terminate such a procedure at any time. It does remain true, however, that when giving is regularized and programmed, the potential for giving increases substantially.

Fourth, evaluate appeals and determine directions of primary interest for your support. As you review your personal philanthropy over the past year and begin this new process, it would seem that several causes that received the lion's share of your philanthropic dollars would benefit the most in increased support as you proceed with philanthropic budget-building. This is not always true, however. Much of our giving is governed by involvement, experience, and impulse. Often, folk discover that the causes most closely aligned to those things most earnestly believed in are not necessarily the causes to which they contribute the most. For example, an individual may be vitally interested in the development of scientific agricultural processes in an area of human society where not only progress but also survival depends on the reality of a program and at least partially available resources to give impact to the effort. The program may be a part of a church's and denomination's structure, and familiarity with the need and objective may be communicated through the local church by the denomination. Because the church is so involved, the individual increases support and considers this a well-defined objective in personal gift procedure. While the contribution to the church is increased in size—the heart of the personal objective being the improvement of skills, agricultural equipment, seed fertilizer, and breed in herd—support is not designated. This project of major concern represents perhaps three-hundredths of 1 percent of the denomination's budget or world assistance program. Increased support to one's church in light of the project stimulating interest and challenging concern actually has little or no impact on the particular situation. The church building is old, the congregation diminished in size, and inflation has influenced the percentage of support going to pastoral ministry, administration, maintenance, and improvements along with fuel for heating, cooling, and lighting. The situation in the local church is repeated in the denomination. The major portion of increased giving is subjected to organizational priorities and necessities, and while interest increases in terms of a project and giving enlarges in terms of need, the effectiveness of the gift is almost nonexistent.

How can one resolve this problem? One holds membership in a particular congregation. The project of greatest concern, a product of the denomination's concern in social-economic-global ministry, becomes known through the church. One can attain one's purpose through designated giving! In the foundation concept, this is called "grantsmanship." Designated support becomes a grant. The donor functions in a manner similar to a foundation executive viewing many proposals, as indeed the donor does, daily, through mass communication media and direct mail. A grant to a cause extends personal concern and accomplishes an important mission at a particular moment in time.

This principle, which is here illustrated through a church, can be illustrated equally well through literally hundreds of membership organizations, nonprofit, approved, and qualifying as legitimate charitable causes—some religious and others secular.

It may well be that one's primary concern is not within the scope of those programs to which a person makes contributions of a major or marginal nature. It may be among those to which minor funding is a fact. How could this be? Unless a person is involved and the appeal for support comes at a truly opportune or convenient time, primary concern may receive modest support.

The foundation concept of budget-building relates to project support—a grant. Both size and potential for the gift increase when we think in terms of programming our giving or support. It is not likely that many personal grants will be one-time gifts. Nor is it likely that gifts of this nature will be programmed over many years. But if the cause is considered deserving and important, the gift may well be programmed over a span of three or four years. The single gift may not seem large, but when it is programmed into budget procedures, it gains in size and significance. A seemingly modest gift takes on real importance as it increases with time repetition. Over three years, a $10-a-month gift becomes $360; a $25 monthly gift over three years becomes $900! Don't smile at this. Remember, the average foundation grant made by the 18,458 foundations having assets under $1 million was $1,799.22 in 1982!

Fifth, consider support for projects that will generate resources beyond your ability to give. "I'll give if you will." This is perhaps the most common statement in financial development for philanthropic causes in the world today. Governments will. Corporations will. Organizations will. Institutions will. People will. On some occasions, for some causes, you must be the first to give. Because you give, others will share generously. Some of the most rewarding experiences in personal philanthropy will come as you take the initiative to begin a process that through the domino effect will stimulate others to give. Governments, corporations, organizations, institutions, and people will give because you cared enough to do the very best you can.

Sixth, monitor your gifts and the projects you support. Some programs will become exciting adventures as you share in tasks and purposes slanted toward the amelioration of human needs. And some, unfortunately, will result in disappointment simply because the task was too great, the resources too limited, or the time inadequate to do what was considered of primary importance when the gift was given. You will sustain support for one, eliminate support for another, and select yet another promising cause as a result of the monitoring process.

It is exciting when you—you and your spouse, or you and your family—consider the actual needs that will demand your attention, challenge your consideration, and stimulate your determination to respond. At this time you will be Santa Claus and champion of your particular world of philanthropy.

As appeals and solicitations are received, they may be filed until the date when the distribution of funds is to be made. By reviewing the appeals and solicitations against funds on deposit for giving, the donor can exercise good stewardship over resources and expend funds wisely. Unprecedented opportunities may well emerge as you become acquainted with other models for creative giving in subsequent chapters.

Giving days will become fun days when you have, in the form of a special bank account, a foundation of your own!

5

Instrumentality
Grantsmanship

The principal of matching funds is an accepted part of our corporate structure in challenge giving, and challenge funding is an important part of philanthropy. At least in its present form, it is a product of World War II. It was then that industry, at the urging of government, sought ways to encourage employees to invest in U.S. war, or savings bonds. In an effort to qualify for an award in excellence, industry challenged employees to purchase savings bonds on a payroll-deduction basis, with the understanding that the employer would match dollar for dollar the amount so designated and paid by the employee.

As the need for war funding decreased and institutions of higher learning with inadequate facilities, limited faculties, and an overrun of students became focal points of concern in national life, many industries responded to this emerging need. Employees—the alumni of literally hundreds of institutions—were now encouraged to respond to their alma maters by making contributions to building funds, expansion programs, and endowments of chairs with the understanding that gifts to qualified institutions would be matched by like amounts by the employing institution. The principle has been extended to hospital and health institutions on the local level by some firms, but almost none have gone so far as to apply it either to organized religion or to most charitable organizations.

Challenge gifts for matching funds, however, have been universally used by educational institutions, religious and secular organizations, as well as national and local charities. Some challenge grants are made by foundations, some by governments, and some by individuals. Major foundations have made grants on the basis that the institution develop resources to match the total sum of the grant in a limited period of time.

The U.S. government through various departments and agencies, as well as state governments, has made grants subject to the provision that municipalities and residents in particular geographic areas raise matching funds. For instance, the Carthage Memorial Hospital was built on the basis that when one-third of the funding had been subscribed by corporations, institutions, and individuals in Hancock County, Illinois, equal sums would be supplied by the State of Illinois and by the federal government.

Individuals, too, provide large gifts for incentive giving with the understanding that their gifts will match dollar for dollar the giving of those sharing in a cause. Sometimes the challenge gift must be met in full by a specified deadline, or the funding opportunity is terminated and no funding is available from that particular challenge source. In other cases, funding is provided as a challenge but with a dollar limit—up to that limit, each dollar the institution or organization is able to raise is matched regardless of the amount.

The basic principle is: "I'll give if you will!"

History does not say who provided the first challenge gift. Many have interpreted the incident in which Jesus fed the five thousand as a chain reaction of unselfishness and sharing in which one small boy began the domino process by giving his five loaves and two fish. This chain reaction, whether or not it offers an adequate explanation of the scriptural incident, is a valid procedure in philanthropy at all levels in society today.

A county was in need of a hospital. The federal and state governments recognized the need for medical services and provided a formula whereby matching funds would be available on the federal and state levels for such facilities if local interest and support could justify the expenditure. A generous resident sensed the need and felt a personal responsibility to develop such a facility in his community. He offered a challenge gift of $500,000 on condition that the residents of the county raise $1 million. His commitment provided the impetus for a successful campaign, which meant that his gift of $500,000 generated gifts of $1 million from residents in the county and grants of $1.5 million each from the state and federal governments.

A church member was interested in encouraging a congregation to develop a bell choir and pledged to purchase one bell for each four bells provided by others, assuming the cost of the largest bell in each of the series of five. In the course of eight months, sixteen people shared, and twenty-five bells were made available for the development of a bell choir in that church.

A church in the Midwest was dedicating a recreational-educational facility. At the open house in connection with the dedication, a parishioner discovered that a youth room had no seating. The building and mortgage obligation had apparently exhausted the congregation's responses. He placed a steel folding chair on a wooden table in the middle of the room and invited those going through the facility to buy a chair. Sixty chairs were purchased with funds provided that day because he was willing to buy the first, thereby becoming an instrument to grantsmanship.

A lodge was nearing the completion of an improvement and decorating program. Unsightly steam registers were necessary to heat the building, and the walls were destined to become dirty as heat forced air up and away from them in wintry months ahead. A lodge member determined to reduce the problem by offering to buy one radiator cover if nine others would accept his challenge and buy one also, thus equipping the entire building. Ten shared as a result of his instrumentality grantsmanship.

Page through the newspapers in our libraries, and you will see incident after incident in which millions have responded to some need arising out of an act of God or a man-made catastrophe. As a result of a favorable response by one, the floodgates of concern and mercy have been opened, and streams of compassion have flown into deserts of hopelessness.

All of these are within the category of instrumentality grantsmanship. They demonstrate that the potential for grantsmanship is available to all—certainly not on the same scale or to the same degree in dollars and cents—but to all in the sense that each person can provide a challenge to creative giving.

Five steps are involved in creative giving in this dimension:

First, one must define his objective. A problem defined is a problem half solved. In the face of a need observed, the potential for new experiments and for devising new means of implementing ideas is beyond human comprehension. There are more ideas than persons. The important task, then, is not only to select a goal but also to define and confine it in such a way that it will seem reasonable and attainable.

The objective should be so defined that if the resources required for the entire program or project are not available, then a reasonable part of the action, or objective, may still be attained with the limited resources that are more immediately available.

A group of professors met at the University of Pennsylvania to outline a project of significance and importance to the university as well as to the cutting edge of human progress in a limited field of activity. The funding required for such a project exceeded $300,000, but there was little likelihood that all would be available from one source at one time. It was suggested that the total project be defined in more limited units. Ultimately, fifteen units were defined that when combined would attain the desired end. No unit was complete by itself. Unless all fifteen units were funded, grants providing for any one or several—even fourteen—could not accomplish the task or move the project toward the desired end. When this flaw was recognized, the group redefined the units in such a way that each was indeed a unit unto itself, and as particular units were funded, progress was made toward the desired end. Consideration must be focused on: What is reasonable? What is feasible? What is attainable?

Second, one must relate his idea or objective to a structure capable of stimulating support and implementing the program. If the idea or objective can relate to a structure with credibility, experience, and capability, it may be attained more readily, and certainly more economically.

In almost every area, there are directories of organizations in which one may find an agency with complementary concerns and sometimes supplementary objectives. Response in support of an idea often is contingent upon tax considerations. Nonprofit organizations are important here.

As an illustration, let us suppose that someone senses a need to provide meals for aged persons confined to their homes. A funding grant of even modest means to a church, synagogue, lodge, club, or organization may stimulate action. Such organizations usually have facilities and people. Their treasuries are equipped to receive and expend funds efficiently and economically, often providing the tax exemption desired and/or required by donors.

A grant commitment providing initial funding and continued funding, although in a somewhat modest dimension, can bring great results. It is amazing how much $100 can do. Like a snowball rolling down a hill, the farther it goes, the larger it grows. To do so, it must be in a proper environment. Snow and hills are a must; structure and organization are essential.

Third, one must make the objective and means of support known. This is simple if the objective is clearly defined and reasonably attainable. Here creditability is important. It cannot be just any church, synagogue, lodge, club, or organization. It must be one with a track record respected in the community, state, or nation; one whose very acceptance of the idea connotes importance, expedience, and credibility.

Nothing is more unfortunate than the marriage of a worthy objective to an incapable or incompatible organization. In these unfortunate unions, there is often fault on both sizes, but too frequently, established organizations are willing to accept funds, even designated, without commitment to purpose.

The means of support also must be simple, convenient, and acceptable to both donor and organization. Many deserving programs limp, falter, and die because channels of support are overly complicated and not readily accessible.

In the world of commerce, what would our pay-up performance be if each consumer had to go to the place of purchase or finance to make payments? Mortgage payments. Car payments. Utility payments. Installment payments. Readily accessible forms with simple remittance envelopes and a convenient depository are the answer, illustrating the principle to which we allude.

Fourth, one must make certain that progress is reported openly, fairly, and honestly. Progress may not be as great as one would hope and the objective in dollars a distance away, but those who share in the objective of the program and have responded to its challenge must be informed. Channels of communication must remain open. Informed people do the right things.

Communication usually is not the task of the person providing "seed money" for an objective. But such persons do have the responsibility to ensure that reporting procedures are established and are regularly performed.

Fifth, one must make sure that the program, whether or not it has attained its objective, is audited in an acceptable manner and that the structure is made accountable to those who have invested of themselves—resources and talents—in making the effort possible.

Instrumentality grantsmanship is a means to creative giving through the marriage of resources and ideas, donors and agencies, money and people.

6

Time, Talent,
and Possessions

It has been a part of our traditional folk-wisdom to say that the "way to a man's heart is through his stomach." Until the Women's Liberation Movement and the Equal Rights Amendment came along, the primary emphasis in the upbringing of daughters was consistent training in the field of domestic engineering. Girls were trained to be housewives and mothers. Akin to this axiom is the realization that the most vital nerve and point of extreme human sensitivity is a person's purse. Fortunately, both concepts are proving to be androgynous in this new age as all develop skills and tastes for fine foods and prove to be equally sensitive to the tug on individual purse strings. When charitable organizations, religious and/or secular, make their appeals, they tug at our purse strings and touch a vital nerve of extreme sensitivity. But the assumption that philanthropy is confined to appeals for financial support and limited to fiscal procedures is entirely false. While financial support is a truly significant part of personal philanthropy, it is only a part, and it is unlikely that the total picture of the philanthropy of even a single individual can be described in monetary terms alone. While we cannot here provide the whole story, we can give attention to at least some of the areas evident in and exercised through many lives.

We might begin with ideas. Every institution has its founders, every organization its founding committee. In each case, some one or some group had an idea. The idea was shared with others, tested

43

in the forge of knowledge, and beat upon the anvil of trial and experience. When duly processed, the institution or organization took birth and became a part of the social-economic-political-spiritual fabric of time. The process is continuous and the experience universal, and no one is excluded from the creative experiment. When one shares ideas, either by intent or circumstance, one is engaged in personal philanthropy.

Before 1950, there was no hospital in Hancock County, Illinois. Serious illness resulting in hospitalization required considerable travel. Patients were transported to Keokuk, Iowa, or Quincy or Macomb, Illinois. The idea took hold that there should be a hospital in that rural county, and the result was Carthage Memorial Hospital.

Before 1955, no home for the aged was provided by Presbyterians in downstate Illinois. With increasing numbers of aging citizens and proportionately fewer facilities, a serious need went unfilled. The idea took hold that there should be a residence for senior citizens in central Illinois, and the result was the Illinois Presbyterian Home.

Before 1960, there was no facility for the training of noninstitutionalized emotionally disturbed, mentally retarded, and/or physically handicapped persons in Orange County, New York. More than five hundred persons were in need of training that would enable them to become semiskilled and independent. The idea took hold that there could be a workshop, and the result was the development of Occupations, Inc., in Middletown, New York.

Visit each of these organizations and you will discover the name of no single individual who is responsible for all that you will find. It took the combined ideas of many individuals to make these communities aware that they could serve vital and important needs right in their midst. Each of us can probably think of similar occasions in which ideas generated in one institution have given birth to other institutions. This is the story of mankind and tends to enhance our understanding of individual membership in the human family as residents in a global village.

While ideas are important to selves, their greater importance is in productivity through social intercourse. No one is an island. No one can live to oneself. Ideas and the cross-fertilization of ideas are very important.

We face difficult problems in the world today, and some of them are receiving the attention of the keenest minds in each culture and nation. But the human predicament worsens with time, and all problems will not be solved by the keenest and best alone. They can only be resolved, and world society more hopefully oriented to the future, if each member of the human race becomes a part of the solution. Each, already, is a part of the problem.

Fortunately, in Western civilization, there are almost an infinite number of opportunities for expressing and sharing ideas. An idea unexpressed and undisclosed is lost potential. At times, one may wonder what to do with an idea—a fleeting thought in a moment in time—and unless initiative is taken to express and share or record the idea, it is lost—lost in time, possibly lost for all eternity.

With whom can ideas be shared? What course can one follow to bring an idea to fulfillment? What can one do with a seemingly good idea?

Seldom, if ever, is an idea unrelated to something else. Ideas are related to products, substances, places, or subjects. Ideas related to products may be shared with manufacturers. Ideas related to substances may be shared with developers and research scientists. Ideas related to places may be shared with those responsible for those places and areas. Ideas related to subjects may be shared with those with a degree of excellence in those subjects.

Institutional and public libraries, magazines, newspapers, radio and television stations—all employ staffs capable of providing points of reference helpful in the documentation, classification, and delivery of ideas. Yellow pages in telephone directories, readily available to every telephone subscriber, provide indices to organizations, institutions, and corporations, as well as people with whom ideas may be shared. In most cases, the deficiency is not in opportunities to express and share ideas but rather in one's neglect of the almost unlimited opportunities available to all. Color, age, race, sex, and nationality know no boundaries here.

Many industries have placed idea or suggestion boxes in strategic locations, and ideas and suggestions are shared by employees and passersby. Sources are sometimes identified and sometimes remain anonymous. Merit systems frequently program methods to reward employees as their ideas and suggestions become part of the productive system, improving the capability of the industry and the productivity and profitability of the particular institution or organization. Personal philanthropy is the sharing of ideas!

Talents in terms of abilities and capabilities may be a part of our philanthropic processes as well.

Recognition procedures have been adopted by many organizations to express appreciation for, and to make known to others, the services that are provided beyond the call of duty and in the areas of voluntary services. The greatest number of those volunteering services and sharing talents do so in connection with organizations that simply do not have the mechanism, capability, or wherewithal to provide such recognition.

A hospital may have a recognition banquet or award ceremony when those serving as "gray ladies" or "candy stripe girls" are recognized with pins, rings, watches, certificates, and titles. An organization may have a recognition banquet or award ceremony where certificates or plaques are given for distinguished services. A college or university may honor a benefactor with a doctorate or citation. For each one recognized in our society today, there will be tens of thousands who are not recognized. Think of those who share in the Marches for Hunger or push doorbells for the United Way; those who stuff envelopes for bulk mailings for the Society for Crippled Children, and those who distribute and collect cans for the March of Dimes; those who serve as Scout leaders, and those who head packs and dens; those who sing in choruses and participate in drama groups; and those who teach in Sunday schools. It is estimated that in the structures of nonprofit organizations throughout the United States there are one hundred and fifty volunteers for every salaried employee. If one were to consider that many provide services to more than one organization, it is very possible that the 1-to-150 ratio might increase to 1 to 300 or even 1 to 1,000. Most organizations in our society could not survive without volunteer service.

The Women's Liberation Movement, with its emphasis on equal rights and self-fulfillment through self-development and vocational proficiency, is making deep inroads into the corps of volunteers that have traditionally been available for all sorts of worthy endeavors. A bright star of promise over the horizon of dismay in this field, however, is that many individuals now have the option of early retirement, with the result that senior citizens today compose an entirely new group from which may be drawn the volunteers needed to provide all sorts of services to humanity.

If dollar values were to be placed on volunteer services, even in terms of minimal salary considerations, we would be overwhelmed with the worth of so great service.

A Philadelphia orthopedic surgeon assumes a volunteer short-term assignment in Jordan to train national physicians there in the science of his speciality. A university student spends an hour a day, three days a week, in a community center to assist "slow learners" in a literacy program. A former insurance salesman residing in a retirement village counsels folk in personal estate planning. The spectrum of human capability is as broad as human need, and all have an opportunity to share. There is simply no end to what people can do in this area, and this is truly a significant aspect of personal philanthropy.

In discussing volunteer services, those who coordinate efforts among volunteers attest that no two persons are alike and each makes a unique and distinctively different contribution to program through service. It is equally true that no two voluntary agencies are alike, and some people may render more effective service in one agency than in another. Individual capability and agency opportunity should be considered carefully when volunteering services.

The Internal Revenue Code provides that necessary costs related to voluntary services may be itemized, thereby qualifying as contributions to charitable and/or religious organizations. It is well for individuals to keep a running account of these costs regardless of whether or not they are declared as contributions. Such an account will permit the person to take inventory of his or her personal philanthropy through the use of talents and evaluate the effectiveness of such gifts of talent. Only in some such fashion may one discover whether or not talents are being utilized in the greatest interest of personal development and of societal needs. One may well discover, in reviewing the past year or decade, that the time has come to change direction, involvement, and objective in order that the utilization of talent may provide the greatest resource possible.

The opportunity to engage in significant volunteer service is by no means limited to those who have dramatic talents to share. During the twelve years of my pastoral ministry in Springfield, Illinois, three classes for mentally retarded children were conducted each day, five days a week, in the church facilities. Most assumed that here were twenty to thirty children and young people who could do nothing. Within weeks, their instructors, through testing and evaluation, discovered that these persons could do some things and that they could do them very well. Almost daily, I was challenged to provide materials that they could use constructively or services they could perform readily. Their talent usually exceeded our ability to discover need. Few times were we able to approach a saturation point. "The Little Drummer Boy" has touched the hearts of millions in Advent Season. Although there appeared to be little the boy could do, few resources he could share, he had his drum and the ability to play it.

Closely related to philanthropy through talents is philanthropy through time. The utilization of talents requires time—for some little, for others much.

Through the years, one of my father's favorite sayings when approached for voluntary services was: "I have more time than money." In childhood years, I thought it a valid statement but have long since come to the conclusion that the statement is false in our twentieth-century society. Of the literally hundreds of funeral services I have conducted through twenty-five years of pastoral ministry, there are perhaps only one or two persons for whom time had not run out before money. In practically every case, the individual's money out distanced his or her time.

No gift one may give is as much discounted or under estimated as time. Few gifts are of greater value. We tend to live busy lives, and the years pass as quickly as the weaver's shuttle. Time is life itself. When one is employed, the employer considers talent in terms of capability and production; and in light of these, it is the person's time that is contracted for, inasmuch as there is no capability or productivity without it. For one, time is of such great value that it is assessed at hundreds of dollars a minute; for others, perhaps only a few cents. There is literally no time without value. And yet no commodity is probably more subject to waste. Of all the gifts of life, few are as subject to neglect and abuse as time.

An instructor of rhetoric assigned class members the task of preparing a calendar allocating time segments over the course of a month in which primary consideration was to be given to certain responsibilities, obligations, and disciplines. It was perhaps the most painful assignment a college student could be given. Impressive is the amount of time literally wasted.

James A. Farley, postmaster general during the administration of the late President Franklin Delano Roosevelt, was asked by a journalist, "How does the president conceive of the world without him?" Farley replied: "Mr. Roosevelt is unable to think of a world without him!" Yet the world turned and society moved perhaps one-third of the time while he was asleep.

Perhaps it is oversimplifying the situation to say that one-third of our time is spent in vocation, one-third in avocation, and one-third at rest. The percentages may vary from individual to individual and during the lifetime for individuals, but all three are important aspects of life and life style.

Examine your day, your days; the year and the years. Apply the philanthropic principle, and determine what elements in time will be used, shared, expended for those matters we tend to assume to be beyond the call of duty.

Budgeting time in terms of philanthropy is as important as budgeting money, and a grant of time may be of greater importance and of greater value than a grant of money or a gift of resources. Time is an important element in personal philanthropy.

When we think of philanthropy, we think too readily in terms of dollars and cents, forgetting that the value of dollars and cents is dependent upon ideas, talents, and time. Concepts and capabilities form the foundation for monetary value. Gold is of no value in and of itself. Its value is determined by the time required to mine, refine, and transport it in comparison with the demand for it. We pay for sweat, callouses, ingenuity—life, in fact—and not for the gold itself.

Commodities and gifts-in-kind are becoming increasingly significant in the private sector even in our urban society. Traditionally these were a part of rural society, where those who could not give a dollar to their church could give a dozen eggs and a chicken to the minister. We are discovering today new ways of sharing manufactured goods and personal possessions. Institutions and organizations have been negligent in making needs known and in structuring means for receiving gifts-in-kind. Some request money of folk who are unable to give financial support. Some request time from those whose calendars and personal responsibilities limit and prohibit their sharing. Some request service from persons whose particular capacity to serve does not match the institutional requirement for service. But commodities, or gifts-in-kind, are legion, and few persons need be excluded from this type of opportunity for sharing.

"One person's junk is another person's wealth." Garage sales, basement sales, porch sales, and tag sales have become a normal part of community life across the nation. Increasingly, our society moves toward a secular nonparticipating society, and items previously provided to rummage sales, charitable auctions, and next-to-new benefit stores are sold directly to provide income to the family purse instead of to an institutional or organizational treasury. In spite of the trend, consider the opportunity one has in our society —the privilege of putting a fair market value upon possessions and receiving credit for them as charitable contributions when given to qualified charitable organizations.

Household items, handicraft products, outgrown and out-of-style clothing, used but good appliances, automobiles, motorcycles, bicycles, and what have you; corn, wheat, barley, oats, and soybeans; cattle, hogs, horses, chickens, and cows; pharmaceutical supplies, manufactured products, and items of surplus and obsolescence in the commercial field can all become a part of personal philanthropy. A friend once said, "I never throw anything away until I have answered the question: Is this something someone else can use?" She seldom discovers a negative answer.

When settling estates, families go through the personal effects of loved ones. When they have completed the task, they sometimes wonder what can be done with those things that remain. Churches, synagogues, lodges, clubs, organizations, and groups will assist you with disposal and provide a credit in the estate ledger, reducing the tax load that is inevitably a part of each estate settlement.

Remove from our catalog of resources the potential of personal philanthropy and you would discover our global village impoverished and consigned to a hopeless future.

7

Property

Philanthropy carries the connotation of contributions, and the usual concept of contributions is direct financial support. An invitation to give is an overture to respond with money. Persons responding to individual and organizational needs do so through cash contributions. A dime for a dog, two bits for a cup of coffee, or a buck for a good cause are common denominators for most Americans. While the majority of contributors share support through dimes, quarters, and dollars, the greater amount of financial support is through bank drafts, securities, plastic currency, and pre-authorized contributions through AUTOGIVE, an electronic funds transfer process, as we emerge into a cashless society.

When we look at the total picture of philanthropy in this country, we may be surprised to discover that a major part of total support is not in cash or even in money of any kind. Sizable giving is in the form of property—property ranging from seemingly insignificant trading stamps to an exquisite work of art by one of the great masters, a bushel of grain to a residence, an article of clothing for a rummage sale to a section of land for development.

Reasons for giving range from disposing of nonessential surplus and obsolescent items to sharing essentials, broadening appreciation for a seemingly priceless treasure, and reaching for recognition and a measure of immortality through gifts of impressive and memorable size. Strange as it may seem on the surface, all of us engage in various elements of sharing that fall into these numerous categories. Much of what we give is not in monetary form, and much of what we can give is without liquidity.

Let us explore those means of giving that may broaden our base of support and enhance our capability and experience in personal philanthropy.

• *First*, there is the area of personal property. Some years ago, I purchased a new pulpit gown, while realizing that there was considerable wear and value in the gown it was to replace. Over several years, I had good intentions of taking the gown to my seminary alma mater in Chicago, where it could perhaps be used by faculty or guests on appropriate occasions. Each time I went to the Windy City, however, it seemed that space in my luggage was at a premium, and continually I fell prey to the temptation to wait and take it next time. The United Presbyterian Church in the U.S.A. included among its publications a biweekly magazine for pastors called *Monday Morning*, and in each issue, there was a section entitled: "For the Asking." Realizing that I would probably never find it convenient to take the robe to Chicago, I decided to offer it, without charge, on a first-come first-served basis, to a clergyman responding to the announcement of its availability in this section of *Monday Morning*. One hundred and three persons responded! This experience made me aware of an interest in used gowns and vestments on a dramatic scale, so I began a project called "Vestment Exchange" in which individuals were invited to contribute a robe, or request a robe, and I would serve as broker for the exchange. More than four hundred vestments have been moved from one clergyman to another in this interesting procedure. Clothing is perhaps the most common item of personal philanthropy.

In a family, clothing moves from person to person. Clothing moves from older children to younger children; from larger persons to smaller persons; from parent to child; from child to parent. Clothing moves from family to kinfolk; from neighbor to neighbor; from individual and family to others beyond the borders of personal encounter. Rummage sales, next-to-new sales, as well as distribution through such organizations as Church World Service, the Salvation Army, Goodwill Industries, and the Volunteers of America move clothing. Millions of tons worth millions of dollars constitute this significant and important component of philanthropy as it spans the nation and encircles the globe.

What has been illustrated through the sharing and use of clothing is valid in terms of most household items ranging from appliances to utensils, furniture to tools, jewelry to incidentals. As we take inventory of our personal possessions, we are impressed that we have a lot to give.

Much of our giving in this area is incidental to our lives and not of primary concern. In most cases, it is giving by necessity—the necessity of getting rid of the "junk," although it may not be junk at all. Through built-in obsolescence, items become disused or outdated because of fashion, style, or need. Take from our culture fabricated obsolescence, and you will destroy a primary basis of our national economy. Manufacturing processes are geared to supply what we desire more than to produce what we need. As fast as one desire is satisfied, a new model comes along, and philanthropy gets a shot in the arm as what has become undesirable to one is handed down to another in need.

Even here we do not tend to exercise as great discipline or prove ourselves as good stewards as we ought or might. Much is consigned to attics and basements to decay or become totally obsolete. Ultimately, it is discarded in the trash heaps of time without recycling in terms of usage or need. Most people overlook a viable asset in charitable giving, not only in the satisfaction that one gains from sharing but also from tax credits as charitable contributions when such contributions are channeled through recognized and qualified organizations and institutions. The gift may be appraised at fair market value, and charitable organizations are in a position to provide valid receipts for merchandise—receipts that are acceptable to the Internal Revenue Service. In fact, even lading costs are recognized as valid portions of the value of a gift.

Items of personal property are not limited to those that have become less important or practical in time. Personal items include things that remain of value and some, indeed, that increase in value with time.

As we visit institutions, galleries, museums, libraries, and public places, we become conscious of this type of gift. Some are of limited value and others of great value. Some are from the personal property inventories of individuals. In some cases, gifts are loaned for a time to be seen and enjoyed by others. An item loaned may represent such value that the offering for use or viewing may constitute a charitable deduction just as in the case of an out-right gift.

Personal gifts have been in the limelight recently because some national leaders have placed value on "personal papers" produced during terms of public office and have consigned them to national or state archives, college or university libraries. In some cases, appraisals have been of inflated value and have been discounted, sometimes disallowed, and on occasion, public figures have been penalized for fraudulent activities in connection with the same. One choosing this course in philanthropy should be exceedingly careful to make certain that the contribution qualifies as a gift and that the property has been properly appraised by qualified persons estimating the value of the gift. These situations are exceptional and should not in any way deter a resolution to be generous and thoughtful of the needs and interests of others.

The following rules are helpful in determining the value of gifts as charitable contributions:

- The value of the gift must be mutually agreed upon by the donor, the recipient, and a qualified and recognized appraiser. The appraiser must be nonpartisan and truly objective in terms of the particular philanthropic process.

- The value of the gift must be consistent with the value of like gifts presented under similar circumstances and so valued by other persons, institutions, and appraisers.

- The documented value of the gift must be acceptable to the Internal Revenue Service.

In presenting gifts of personal property, one should rise above the expedient and convenient to discover, insofar as possible, the greatest benefit one can provide through sharing. Much of our giving is sporadic and sentimental. And for numerous institutions, this may be just as well. One cannot always exercise one's best judgment or attain the perfect good. One should assess the value of the gift to the donor, the value of the gift to the institution, and the value of the gift to the particular community. The value of the gift to posterity is an important consideration as well.

On one occasion, a small college in central Illinois received a gift that had sentimental value both for the donor and for the faculty. Unfortunately, arrangements required for the utilization of the gift were so costly that the gift became a liability instead of an asset.

Strictly in terms of dollars, it would have been wiser for the institution to refuse the gift. A greater service would have been for the institution to redirect the gift to a place where it would be an asset instead of a liability and ultimately yield greater satisfaction to all involved.

One should remember that no gift is a gift unto itself. Every gift, whether large or small, apparently significant or insignificant, imposes a responsibility and obligation on the receiving organization. In cash gifts, we have discovered that contributions under $14.69 are not gifts at all. So also with gifts of personal property. The care of the gift during the time it is included in the inventory of the institution requires unavoidable expenses in terms of space, maintenance, insurance, and so on. Persons making gifts should carefully evaluate these factors.

Real property may also be a significant source of philanthropic giving. Often we think of gifts of this type in terms of wills and bequests. Increasingly, they appear in institutional reports as important components in the world of philanthropy today. The Harriman estate in New York and the Robert Allerton estate in Illinois are classic examples. The Harriman estate is now a conference center for Columbia University and the Robert Allerton estate a conference center for the University of Illinois. We need not think of real estate in terms of a truly large estate when we consider philanthropic giving. Travel up and down the streets in almost any community and you will find residences converted into offices, neighborhood houses, halfway houses, and other types of insitutions as they have been deeded to qualified charitable organizations or institutions. The properties in terms of age, size, and location are no longer practical as individual family residences, and their design has been changed to meet the needs of organizational or institutional life. We need not confine our thinking to the historical past in communities to see title transfers of deeded property to religious and charitable organizations. In this age of condominiums, it may surprise some to discover the number of apartments that have been deeded to charitable organizations as an economy move in a difficult period of inflation, increased taxes, and limited incomes, with donors reserving the right of occupancy for as long as they live or are able to maintain the facility themselves.

Consider the gift of real property as an outright gift to an institution or organization. The property constitutes a gift equal to its value in the current market. When property is provided as a basis for a gift annuity or charitable remainder trust, the value of the gift for the institution issuing the annuity or trust agreement is determined by the amount of money the institution or organization actually receives from the sale of the property. This would represent the proceeds from the sale of the property reduced by the costs of attorney's fees, taxes, insurance, and so on. One might ask: Why not sell the property outright and give the money to the institution or organization instead? Under current Internal Revenue Code provisions, this would be inadvisable inasmuch as inflation and increased value would impose taxes on capital gains. Charitable organizations and charitable institutions are excluded from them. Note the following illustration.

Sally Smith is interested in giving her home to a recognized charity in exchange for an annuity. She and her husband bought the home at the time it was constructed for $4,700. The home, although twenty years old, has a market value of $43,000. Unless money from the proceeds of the sale were invested in another residence within a twenty-four-month period of time, capital gains subject to taxation would amount to $38,300. In actuarial return from the charitable organization, she may expect to receive $24,000 from the annuity over a period of years. Inasmuch as capital gains are assessed on the difference between the original cost of the property to the donor and the actuarial value of the annuity, capital gains on this gift will total $19,300. She has avoided $23,700 in capital gains by deeding the property to the charitable organization in exchange for an insured annual income to continue for as long as she lives. If, however, the property is given outright, without the benefit of an annuity or trust income, there are no capital gains whatsoever, and the entire value constitutes a charitable contribution for tax purposes.

Sally Smith has still another option. She may contribute the property to a charitable institution, and her charitable deduction will be based on the number of years she may be expected to occupy the property and/or the number of years she may be expected to live after the consummation of the gift.

The advantages to Sally of these procedures are:

- The gift value of the deeded property may be declared as a contribution in the year in which the agreement is made, with a carry-over for as many as five succeeding years. Her income tax schedules may be such that this would be an exceedingly wise procedure to follow.
- In the event of her death, the property is no longer a part of her estate inasmuch as it has been deeded to a charitable organization and is therefore not subject to estate taxes.
- In the event that the value of the property increases over the remainder of her lifetime, there are no capital gains to affect her or her estate at the time of her demise. As was stated earlier, the owners of condominiums increasingly are utilizing this procedure to assist them in their retirement and in reducing the tax burden to their incomes and to their estates.

In pursuing this course, you may find that some charitable organizations will not be willing to receive your gift. In some cases, they will require that funds be placed in escrow to insure the payment of taxes, repairs, and upkeep in order that the institution or organization not be involved economically or morally in the upkeep of the property and the payment of taxes. No organization is likely to become a party to any such charitable procedure unless the property ensures income on a deferred basis to the organization and makes few or no demands for staff or funding that the organization may well not be able to afford.

Many properties are offered to charitable organizations and refused simply because they would be liabilities instead of assets. Literally hundreds of millions of dollars in property would be deeded immediately to organizations from large, deteriorating metropolitan areas were the organizations willing to receive them. If properties are not marketable, or if they do not lend themselves to valuable usage, they simply will not, and should not, be accepted as gifts.

Real estate—improved and unimproved; urban, suburban, and¢rural—constitutes a significant part of American philanthropy and may increasingly do so as inflation swirls in an upward spiral; as taxes increase with greater demands for municipal, state, and federal services; and as incomes for the retirement group remain basically the same or proportionately less in terms of inflation and increased tax burden.

Gifts of property, personal and real, are significant options with desirable benefits as one structures a blueprint for philanthropy in the future.

8

Gift Annuities

Over many years, the Gift Annuity has provided an opportunity for personal philanthropy in the American way of life. The Salvation Army probably services more and benefits more from annuity contracts than any single organization on this continent. Gift Annuities are not by any means limited to national organizations, however, colleges, universities, seminaries, prep schools, and literally hundreds of organizations qualify as capable of issuing and servicing annuity agreements.

What are the advantages of an annuity agreement for an individual? Here is an illustration:

Robert Brown at age 82 presents securities having a market value of $10,000 to his favorite charity. In return, he will receive the sum of $1,020 a year for as long as he lives. Income may be programmed at his option in an annual payment of $1,020, two semi-annual payments of $510, four quarterly payments of $255, or twelve monthly payments of $85 each year for as long as he lives.

Four distinct benefits result from this procedure in charitable giving:

First, Robert Brown has entered into an agreement with $10,000 worth of securities that under the rules of the Internal Revenue Service are recognized as having a gift value in the amount of $5,305.96. This sum may be declared as a charitable contribution in the year in which the agreement is written or carried over as many as five succeeding years. Income, taxes, and limitations on the amount of charitable deduction that may be taken in any one year may well determine the amount.

Second, having elected to receive payments annually, of the $1,020 that Robert Brown receives each year, he has an exclusion of 74.2 percent for tax purposes. In other words, of the $1,020 that he receives each year, only $263.16 is taxable income.

Third, inasmuch as Robert Brown provided appreciated securities in negotiating the Gift Annuity contract, his capital gains are limited to the actuarial value of the agreement, which is based on life expectancy instead of the face value of the agreement, and this actuarial figure is the modest sum of $4,694.04. In the event the securities originally cost less than $4,694.04, his capital gains would constitute the difference between the purchase price and the actuarial figure. In the event the purchase price exceeded the actuarial value, there would be no capital gains whatsoever.

Fourth, because the capital provided for the Gift Annuity is given to a qualified charitable organization, the asset is no longer a part of Robert Brown's estate and will not be subject to estate taxes at the time of his demise.

The schedules on the facing page will be helpful in understanding the income and tax factors in annuity agreements.

Gift Annuities are most attractive to the 65-year-old and older group. For those at middle age, Gift Annuities should be contracted for on a deferred income basis. Since September 1972, religious and charitable organizations have been permitted to issue such annuity contracts under a revision in the Internal Revenue Code.

A person of any age may enter into an annuity agreement with a qualified charitable organization, providing a gift now and a tax-sheltered income beginning at a designated date. As an illustration: Mary Brown, aged 45 years, contributes $10,000 to her favorite charity. At age 65, she is to receive an annual income of 16.1 percent, or $1,610, each year for as long as she lives. The gift value of the agreement is $4,624.20, and she may declare this as a gift in the year in which the agreement is made with a carry-over for as many as five succeeding years. Of the $1,610 she will receive each year beginning at age 65, she will have a tax exclusion on her annual income of approximately 25.5 percent under the present terms of

TABLE 3. THE GIFT ANNUITY CONTRACT
(Based on quarterly payments)

Age	Rate (%)	Gift value (%)	Tax-free income (%)
		MALE	
60	7.0	18.9	63.9
65	7.3	24.3	68.7
70	7.8	31.8	72.8
75	8.5	39.0	75.4
80	9.6	46.2	75.6
85	11.4	52.6	74.2
		FEMALE	
60	7.0	12.3	57.9
65	7.3	17.3	62.5
70	7.8	22.3	66.7
75	8.5	28.3	70.2
80	9.6	34.2	72.0
85	11.4	39.6	71.5
		TWO LIVES	
60/60	6.6		
65/65	6.8		
70/70	7.1		
75/75	7.6		
80/80	8.3		
85/85	9.4		

In determining age, figure from nearest birthday.
Uniform Gift Annuity Rates adopted by Conference on Gift Annuities, May 5, 1983.

the Internal Revenue Code. Her taxable annual income from the annuity will be approximately $1,206.90.

In the event that appreciated securities are contributed as a basis for the Deferred Payment Gift Annuity, the capital gains are measured against the actuarial value, as in a regular Gift Annuity contract; but the assessment is programmed over the years in which annuity payments are received, and a very small portion is computed as taxable income each time.

An additional illustration (Table 4) may be helpful: Mae Jones, aged 55 years, entered into a Deferred Payment Gift Annuity agreement with securities valued at $10,000. She originally purchased the securities for $5,000; however, because the securities have provided a base for a Deferred Payment Gift Annuity, she pays no capital gains until she reaches the age of 65 years, when her annuity income begins, and the gains will be assessed at $136.50 a year for as many as 17.7 years. If she dies before she reaches the age of 82.7 years, the gains not yet reported are forgiven.

Viewing the benefits for individuals and couples in the Gift Annuity program for those over 65 years of age with benefits beginning immediately, and on a deferred income basis for those under 65 years of age, one may well ask: What is the benefit to the institution?

The benefit to the organization or institution will be determined by investment procedures, inflation, and, of course, the sex and age of the donor or donors.

If the charitable organization is self-insured and retains the asset in its investment portfolio, the organization may receive considerably more than the face value of the agreement. Let us suppose that the donor's return on the Gift Annuity is 7 percent. If the investment portfolio keeps pace with the inflationary spiral, and the annual income from the investment in the portfolio would total 6 percent, the residual of the investment, growth, and income may exceed the amount required for the donor's income by 8 to 12 percent. Actuarials are structured on the basis that in a static-ordinary market an institution will receive at a minimum 50 percent of the contract for its program. Few contracts result in gifts so modest.

If the organization is not self-insured and it has negotiated a contract with an insurance company to insure the donor's income for as long as the donor lives, the organization may receive 50 to 80 percent of the gift for the current program. The risk under these

TABLE 4. DEFERRED PAYMENT GIFT ANNUITY

A. GUARANTEED DEFERRED ANNUITY RATES (MALE AND FEMALE)

Present age	Age when payments begin	Rate of annual income (%)
45	60	12.7
45	65	16.1
50	65	13.2
50	70	17.2
55	65	10.8
55	70	14.1
60	65	8.7
60	70	11.5
65	70	9.3

B. PORTION OF GIFT QUALIFYING AS A CONTRIBUTION

Present age	Age when payments begin	Percentage of contribution a gift	
		Male	Female
45	60	40.9	34.3
45	65	53.4	46.2
50	65	48.0	40.3
50	70	60.7	52.3
55	65	41.4	33.4
55	70	55.6	46.6
60	65	24.0	17.0
60	70	49.3	39.8
65	70	41.2	31.5

C. TAX-FREE PORTION OF ANNUAL INCOME

Present age	Age when payments begin	Projected tax-free income (%)	
		Male	Female
45	60	26.2	24.3
45	65	19.9	18.8
50	65	27.1	25.5
50	70	19.6	19.1
55	65	37.4	34.8
55	70	27.1	26.0
60	65	60.2	53.8
60	70	37.9	36.0
65	70	54.4	50.7

TABLE 4, cont.

D. DEFERRED PAYMENT GIFT ANNUITY (TWO LIVES)

Husband's age	Wife's age	Number of years before payments begin	Rate of annual income (%)
45	40	15	11.8
50	45	15	12.2
55	50	10	10.0
60	55	5	8.0
65	60	5	8.2

E. PORTION OF GIFT QUALIFYING AS A CONTRIBUTION ON TWO LIVES AGREEMENTS

Husband's Age	Wife's Age	Number of years before payments begin	Percentage of contribution a gift
45	40	15	14.09
50	45	15	29.64
55	50	10	22.34
60	55	5	14.28
65	60	5	22.13

conditions is assumed by the insurance procured by the organization to insure the donor's annual income.

One may further ask: What is the risk factor in Gift Annuity programs? Annuity contracts are subject to statutes on both the federal and state levels that require reporting procedures by agencies issuing annuity contracts to ensure the agencies' capability of meeting the terms of the contract for the security of the donor and to protect the donor's interest. Laws and procedures governing insurance companies govern the charitable organizations as well. For all practical purposes, one may assume a Gift Annuity contract to be as reliable and as valuable as an insurance policy providing comparable lifetime income.

Statutes governing Gift Annuities vary from state to state. In some states, institutions are not permitted to issue Annuity contracts; however, the state laws governing a contract are those in which a particular institution or organization is chartered, rather than those of the state in which the donor lives. A New York-based institution may issue contracts to donors in all fifty states regardless of the particular statutes governing institutions in the state in which the donor lives.

Almost without exception, Gift Annuity contracts are written for the benefit of the institution issuing the contract. But, many denominations have foundations that will issue contracts in which a local church, or church-related institution, may share on a fifty-fifty basis. The National Consultation on Financial Development is unique in that it will issue an Annuity contract for the benefit of any qualified religious or charitable organization, providing immediate benefit to the organization so designated. Its procedure is to reinsure the agreement to provide income sufficient to meet the terms of the contract and provide the donor's insured benefit. The balance, usually ranging from forty to sixty percent, never leaves the treasury of the organization or organizations benefiting from the contract. While the guidelines under which the National Consultation writes such contracts are intentionally broad, it would be reasonable to assume the National Consultation would not issue a contract for the benefit of an institution or organization whose purposes are inconsistent with the National Consultation's own charter. Always recognizing these limitations, interested persons may address inquiries to the National Consultation on Financial Development, 31 Langerfeld Road, Hillside, N.J., 07642 (201 664-8890).

A Gift Annuity on a current or deferred payment basis is a form of philanthropic giving that deserves to be more widely known and used. It provides funding for charitable organizations, tax shelters, and hedges against inflation. In addition, it offers the possibility of a substantial reduction in taxation through the charitable deduction, the avoidance of a tax on capital gain, an annual exclusion from the individual's income tax, and the elimination of at least that portion from estate taxes.

9

Charitable Remainder Trusts

The Charitable Remainder Trust is an increasingly common tool utilized by many in support of qualified religious and charitable organizations, especially as individuals discover the procedure and the fact that they may establish a trust, define the terms, and name the organization or organizations as remaindermen without the knowledge of the institutions or organizations involved. Processes have been streamlined, in some cases, to enable those of comparatively modest means to establish trusts with sums as small as $5,000. Until recent years, only those who could invest as much as $100,000 could consider the trust route for charitable giving. Now the thoroughfare is open to almost all.

In *New Models for Financing the Local Church*, I outlined five types of situations in which Charitable Remainder Trusts are most attractive. Let us look at them now:

- *Situation One.* A highly successful businessman is in his mid-forties. His annual income has increased to six figures, placing him in a high tax bracket. Over the past dozen years, he has invested in an impressive portfolio of securities. Because of the capital gains factor, he is hesitant to make revisions in the portfolio; and as a result, his potential capital growth will become increasingly limited in the future in a reinvestment program. He is vitally interested in his church. This interest, added to the burden of his investment concern, provides a most desirable answer for both him and his church. He establishes an irrevocable charitable trust that pays him a modest income until he reaches the age of 65 years, after which it provides a higher income during his retirement years. It also provides him with tax-exclusion benefits for the rest of his life. His estate tax picture, too, is greatly improved, and the residual of the investment becomes the asset of his church at his demise.

• *Situation Two.* An attorney suggests to a widow that she proceed with estate planning. He recommends that she take $25,000 of appreciated securities and establish a trust. An officer of her church serves as trustee because the residual in the trust will go to the church at the time of her death. Her first approach to designing a trust agreement is to contact the trust department of her local bank. Here she is discouraged because the institution will not handle a trust agreement in which assets are under $100,000. The trustee in the local church, representing the board of trustees of the church, through the counsel of a qualified investment broker, places the assets in an open-end investment company that can handle investment portfolios as small as $5,000. This trust agreement provides her with an immediate tax deduction, an exclusion on a sizable portion of the annual income, a sizable tax benefit for her estate at the time of her death, and the capital remaining becomes an asset of her church when she dies.

• *Situation Three.* A couple in their early retirement years discover that they are property poor. Most of their resources are in real estate, and their liquid assets are extremely limited. They put some of their real estate, representing $100,000, in trust. The trust sells the real estate without being required to pay taxes on the appreciated value, invests the proceeds from the sale in securities providing a reasonable return, and pays the donors $8,000 a year for as long as either shall live. The couple reduce their real estate tax burden, have a benefit in a charitable contribution that may equal 50 percent of their income with carry-over for several years, have an exclusion on a portion of their annual income for as long as either lives, and will have a distinct advantage in tax shelter on their real estate when either or both die. The residual of the trust will be a distinct asset for their church and provide a meaningful memorial for family members and friends for many years to come.

• *Situation Four*. A gentleman has been most successful in his business enterprises and is due for retirement in three years. He wants to maximize his retirement income without incurring capital gains taxes on his appreciated securities. Also, he wants to provide adequately for his wife should he die. He, too, consults with his attorney and the trustees of his local church. A special trust is established providing a comfortable income for him and his wife. His federal estate tax liability is greatly reduced, and he and his wife annually have income tax deductions as a result of the trust. When they both die, the residual will go to their local church.

• *Situation Five*. This gentleman was fortunate in buying early in his business career a block of securities that gained in value to almost unbelievable proportions. Because the securities are of the growth type, the annual income is very small. He would like to sell them and place the money received in high-yielding securities; however, the capital gains taxes would be crushing. He and his attorney consult the trustees of his local church. He establishes a trust agreement whereby the securities are irrevocably given to the local church to be invested for his benefit. The trust is written so that it will provide him with an annual income of $10,000 a year. The low-yield income securities are sold by the trustee, who may be a trustee of the local church as well, and there is no capital gain. The donor's annual income has a sizable tax exclusion. At his demise, the assets from the trust belong to the local church.

There are three types of trust agreements.

First, the Charitable Remainder Annuity Trust. The Charitable Remainder Annuity Trust provides an annual income governed by the terms of the trust agreement, and the annual income never varies. The annual return to the donor, or donors, does not depend upon either the return to the trust from investment procedures or the capital gains for the investment. In the event that income and gains do not equal the amount required for the annuity payment to the individual, or individuals, the amount required will be withdrawn from capital. In the event that both gains and income exceed the amount required for the annuity payments to the donor, or donors, the income in excess of need is retained in the trust and ultimately accrues to the benefit of the institution or organization, institutions or organizations, as remaindermen in the trust agreement. The Internal Revenue Code prescribes that the rate of annual return shall exceed a floor of 5 percent. In the event a Charitable Remainder Annuity is established for $10,000 with the annual annuity income designated at 5 percent, the annual income to the donor will be $500; 6 percent, $600; 7 percent, $700; 8 percent, $800; 9 percent, $900; and 10 percent, $1,000. The return, defined by the terms of the trust, will never vary.

Second, The Charitable Remainder Trust. The Charitable Remainder Trust provides an annual return based upon the market value of the funds in trust at the anniversary of the establishment of the trust. The floor, also determined by the Internal Revenue Code, is 5 percent. The annual income to the donor will vary with market conditions, and the person, or persons, establishing the trust will determine whether or not they are willing to take a risk in terms of the amount of annual income.

There is no risk in terms of the Charitable Remainder Annuity Trust, but there may be risk in terms of the Charitable Remainder Trust—risk in terms not of income but of amount of income that will result annually from the trust. The risk may be that of more limited income in certain years because of unfavorable market conditions affecting the value of the invested funds constituting the trust. Table 5 may be helpful in understanding the procedure.

At the expiration of the trust, which comes at the demise of the individual, or individuals, benefiting from the trust, the institution or organization, institutions or organizations, receive the capital funds held in trust. In the above case, should the trust terminate at the twentieth anniversary, the sum would be $145,000. In the event the trust were a Charitable Remainder Annuity Trust and the market conditions similar to those listed in the table above, the institution, or institutions, would receive considerably more because not only the rate of return but also the income each year would be fixed at the $5,000 level, and income to the trust exceeding the required payout for the annuity would accrue to the benefit of the institution, or institutions, as remaindermen of the trust. In the illustration above, it is possible that the institution might receive as much as $250,000!

TABLE 5. DOLLAR INCOME FROM A CHARITABLE REMAINDER TRUST*		
Value of trust (in dollars)	Rate of return (%)	Income (in dollars)
Initial investment — 100,000	5	5,000
1st anniversary — 102,500	5	5,125
2nd anniversary — 99,000	5	4,950
3rd anniversary — 95,000	5	4,500
4th anniversary — 101,000	5	5,050
5th anniversary — 105,000	5	5,500
10th anniversary — 120,000	5	6,000
15th anniversary — 106,000	5	5,600
20th anniversary — 145,000	5	7,250

*Related to hypothetical fluctuations in market value of trust funds.

Third, the Unitrust. The Unitrust may be a Charitable Remainder Annuity Trust or a Charitable Remainder Trust, but it will differ from the two as discussed above in that the benefiting institution, or one of the benefiting institutions, will share in the trust procedure by serving as trustee. In this event, the funds establishing the trust are given irrevocably to the institution, and they are invested in the commingled account of the institution for the period of the trust agreement. The terms of the trust may be such that more than one institution may benefit as remaindermen, but only one institution will serve as trustee for the trust funds. While trust funds are invested in a commingled account, accounting procedures will convert the initial value of the trust into shares, and the trust will maintain its identity in share value and not in dollar value. The value of the shares will vary with the market, of course, but no particular block of investments as such will represent the funds constituting the trust.

A number of rules govern procedures for Charitable Remainder Trusts:

• The rate of return to the donor, or donors, must equal or exceed 5 percent per annum.

• The remaindermen must be qualified and recognized charitable institutions as defined by Section 501(c)(3) of the Internal Revenue Code.

• The minimum size of the trust will vary from institution to institution, organization to organization, and trustee to trustee. Banking institutions generally will not manage a trust agreement consisting of less than $100,000. Organizations and institutions may manage trust accounts of sums as modest as $5,000. The National Consultation on Financial Development is unique in that it will counsel in the management of trust accounts as modest as $5,000 and will serve as trustee for such accounts when there is more than one remainderman. It requires, however that no less than 20 percent of the funds remaining at the termination of the trust be designated for the National Consultation on Financial Development as unrestricted funds, or designated for a program or project to which it relates.

• In establishing the trust, the donor, or donors, relinquish control of the funds in trust. Reports from the trustee will be provided to the donor at least annually; however, the donor has no power to advise or govern the trustee in the management of the trust or investment of the funds held in trust. Perhaps this is best understood when one realizes that the trustee's primary function is to protect the interest of the institution or the organization as remainderman. This is implied in the very title of the agreement, namely, Charitable Remainder Trust.

• Costs involved in the management of the portfolio, the purchase and sale of securities, and the reporting procedure are borne by the trust.

• The gift value of the trust agreement is determined at the time the trust is established, and the gift may be reported as a charitable contribution for income tax purposes in the year in which the trust is established or, at the time of this writing, programmed over as many as five succeeding years under provisions of the Internal Revenue Code.

• Regardless of the value of the shares or funds held in trust, no benefit accrues to the individual in terms of capital gains. The funds no longer are an asset or liability of the donor or donors, but rather of the charitable institution or institutions, organization or organizations, designated in the trust.

• The tax exclusion on the annual income is determined by the sex and age or sexes and ages of the person or persons benefiting from the trust.

• The gift value, as well as the exclusion on annual income, is determined by the age or ages of the individual or individuals involved and the rate of return established for same. The more advanced the age and the more modest the annual return (5 instead of 8 percent as an illustration), the greater the benefits in terms of taxes and tax exclusion on annual income.

• The remainderman or remaindermen must be qualified and recognized charitable organizations as defined by Section 501(c)(3) of the Internal Revenue Code. In the event that the charity ceases to function, the successor organization will be the ultimate beneficiary. If no successor organization exists, the donor or donors who established the trust may designate another organization as remainderman, and if that organization dissolves after the death of the donor and previous to the distribution of the funds in trust, the trustee will determine the organization to receive the funds. Court procedures will ensure that the use of the funds is consistent with the intention of the donor, or donors, in establishing the trust.

Here are some significant points to remember:

Charitable Remainder Trusts may be established with sums as modest as $5,000.

Persons establishing trusts determine the terms of the trust within parameters established by the Internal Revenue Code.

Funds may remain in trust for the lifetime of the donor or those benefiting from the trust, or for a designated period of time (e.g., twenty years).

Charitable Remainder Trusts may be established without the knowledge of the institution or organization, institutions or organizations, benefiting from the trust except in the case of the Unitrust, in which case the trustee is named by an institution and the funds in trust assimilated in the commingled investment portfolio of the institution.

Specimen forms for the Charitable Remainder Trust and the Charitable Remainder Annuity Trust are available from trust companies, the trust departments of commercial banks, and the National Consultation on Financial Development. Your legal counsel and/or trust officer is in a position to provide information about requirements for establishing a trust in your state. Persons establishing trusts may choose a state other than that in which they reside or in which the benefiting institution or institutions are located if they wish. It is expedient to obtain the services of qualified legal counsel in setting up all such trusts to make certain that proper procedures are followed and to ensure maximum benefits both for the donor or donors and the institution or institutions designated as the eventual beneficiaries.

Individuals will do well to consider the Charitable Remainder Trust route for personal philanthropy. It provides one of the most creative models for giving in that it is designed completely by the donor and may be established without the assistance or knowledge of the institution or organization ultimately to benefit from the trust. And the donor determines the rate of annual return needed to care for personal and family needs. The trust is a truly fine opportunity for major contributions.

10

Life Insurance Policies

Seldom does the average person think of life insurance as a significant aspect of personal philanthropy other than in estate planning,
when listing assets to determine the distribution of those that may
remain following death. In some cases, insurance policies have
simply been overlooked in estate planning. Policies include the redesignation of beneficiaries as family situations change through
marriage, maturity, sometimes divorce and death. In some cases,
when the insured is bereft of kin or friend, the beneficiary named
is a charitable or religious organization. Frequently, those making
such designations do not realize that tax advantages provided by
the Internal Revenue Code are of immediate benefit to the individual when the institution is named irrevocably as beneficiary. If
the designation is specified as an irrevocable one, the individual
may declare the designation in his or her report, or tax return, to
the Internal Revenue Service as a gift in an amount equal to the
sum that would be required to replace that particular insurance
policy at the particular time the irrevocable designation is made. It
should be emphasized that the gift value is not the "cash sur-
render" value or even the "paid-up insurance" value of the policy.
Generally, the contribution value will equal the cost-basis of the
policy.

There are times when such designations will exceed the amount
permissible to declare as contributions in the particular year
the designation is made. In that event, undeclared portions of

charitable contributions exceeding 50 percent of the adjusted gross income may be carried over to as many as five succeeding years.

This is an opportunity overlooked by most persons. Many do not consider designating irrevocably as the beneficiary of a policy a qualified religious or charitable organization as responsibilities and obligations change with families raised, dependents becoming independent, and loved ones dying.

It has been stated that the designation must be irrevocable to qualify as a valid contribution at the time of designation. This is true to the extent that the beneficiary must be a recognized and registered charitable organization qualified as such in terms of Section 501(c)(3) of the Internal Revenue Code. Once the designation is made, it it not possible to redesignate a family member, friend, or nonqualifying cause as the beneficiary. It is possible, however, to designate another qualifying organization as the beneficiary. As an example: An individual living in New York City may name the local chapter of the Society for Crippled Children as the beneficiary of his or her insurance policy. At a later date, because of relocation or a restructuring of priorities or basic concerns, the person may wish to redesignate the beneficiary to be the Sloane-Kettering Cancer Research Center at Rye, New York. This is permissible. Perhaps a more realistic illustration would be the instance of a person designating as beneficiary the Old Stone Presbyterian Church in Cleveland, Ohio, and later redesignating as beneficiary the Presbyterian Church by the Sea in Fort Lauderdale, Florida. The key is simply that the designation provide aid to a qualified organization in the United States of America.

An accompanying benefit to the irrevocable beneficiary designation for a qualified religious or charitable organization in the United States is that the policy is no longer an asset to be considered a part of the individual's estate. A fringe benefit established through the designation is the reduction of taxable worth in settling the estate.

Insurance programs have been utilized by eleemosynary organizations from time to time as fund-raising procedures, as well.

Group life insurance has been arranged by officers of charitable organizations providing for participation by individual "members" in the organization. In some cases, the criteria for membership include little more than one's willingness to share in such an

insurance program. One such member will enroll, and the enroll-
ment will consist of an application for participation in the group
insurance program in sums ranging from $500 to $500,000. The
group policy includes a mandatory provision that the beneficiary
be irrevocably the particular organization or agency in which the
person takes membership. The option, discussed previously, providing for a redesignation from one qualified charitable organization to another is no longer possible. The individual applies for the
policy, and it is his or her moral responsibility to pay for the policy
on a monthly, quarterly, semiannual, or annual basis. Inasmuch as
the policy is irrevocably designated for the benefit of the qualified
charitable organization, the funds paid by the individual in payment of premiums are eligible for credit as a charitable contribution
by the Internal Revenue Code.

As increased numbers of persons hold membership and share in
the insurance program, the organization may use the insurance
policy, or policies as the case may be, for collateral in borrowing
funds to build, enlarge, or improve the organization's facilities.
Repayment of the indebtedness is attained in one of several ways.

•   The dividends provided by the insurance policy provide
quarterly or annual income. This may be used in payment of the
principal on the indebtedness incurred by the organization. We are
assuming, in this event, that the policy has been recently implemented, and borrowing for building, enlarging, or improvement
has been arranged with banking institutions perhaps in the area of
the organization.

•   If the policy has been in force for a considerable period of
time, and equity established through group participation, the organization may borrow from the insurance company at minimum interest rates. The sum would equal the loan value of the policy. On
each anniversary, the loan value increases. When an organization
has financed initial facilities from a commercial firm, it is possible
that the annual increase in loan value, together with dividends,
will make possible the full payment of the debt amortization program of the organization.

•   The incidence of mortality provides considerable benefit in
this program as well. Suppose one is considering the support the
eventual beneficiary of his philanthropy will enjoy, one might
ask: How far is a project from money in such situations? The

estimate of income is based on the age and sex of the participants as they relate to the mortality rate.

Suppose we project income for groups of one hundred persons in which each participant will be required to share to the extent of purchasing $5,000 in insurance for the benefits of an organization. The income will vary according to the age and composition of the group:

- If the participants range in age from 20 to 100 years and consist of both female and male members, the insurance can be expected to provide $15,000 a year. If the group is entirely female, insurance will provide only $10,000 a year, and if the group is entirely male, insurance will provide as much as $20,000 a year.

- If the participants range in age from 40 to 100 years and consist of both female and male members, the insurance can be expected to provide $20,000 a year. If the group is entirely female, insurance will provide only $15,000 each year, and if the group is entirely male, insurance will provide as much as $25,000 a year.

- If the participants range in age from 60 to 100 years and consist of both female and male members, the insurance can be expected to provide $70,000 a year. If the group is entirely female, insurance will provide only $47,000 a year, and if the group is entirely male, it will provide as much as $93,000 a year.

Individuals may consider enrolling in programs of this type supporting organizations and institutions in which they have a vital and vibrant interest. Usually, organizations so constituted will make these opportunities known to you.

Indeed, on occasion, one might become a pioneer in organizing and establishing such a program to cope with a basic problem or concern. Such an effort must be administered by a qualified charitable or religious organization. And there is also the possibility, in a truly pioneering endeavor, that a corporate structure may have to be established to accommodate the program. In this event, qualified legal counsel will be required, and the statutes of the particular state in which the corporation is formed, as well as the Internal Revenue Code, will provide the matrix for the organization, management, and functional elements necessary to furnish the service and attain the desired objective.

It is important to remember that in programs of this type funds paid for insurance qualify as contributions to charitable causes, and there is no tax involvement whatever at the demise of the individual to affect the estate or the organization named irrevocably as the beneficiary.

11

Wills and Bequests

"I do not have a will!"

This is a common statement in our society. It is also false. The truth of the matter is that everyone has a will. Regardless of age or circumstance, state arbitrary intestacy laws govern the distribution of a person's real and personal property in the event that no other document is available to determine an individual's designation for the disposal of real and personal property at his or her demise.

In the North American Interchurch Study, a survey of some 3,500 individuals in the United States and Canada conducted in 1971, 56 percent of the clergy and 44 percent of the laity interviewed indicated that they did not have wills. There are other studies indicating that as many as 97 percent of the American people do not have wills. Probably a valid estimate would fall somewhere between the 44 percent of the church-related laity and the 97 percent reported in some studies.

Obviously, more people are making wills today than did so a generation ago. A century ago, it was common for persons to have wills. Property owners considered a will of equal importance to the title or deed to their property. Now religious and charitable organizations are making a greater thrust in this area of philanthropy, and certainly, it is paying off. Yet, they have failed in the area of wills. In 1963, bequests represented 8.3 percent of American philanthropy, and in 1983 they represented 7.0 percent of American philanthropy. A decrease of 15.6 percent in twenty-one years. People are not "will conscious." Only a very few take advantage of the opportunity the making of a will provides for designating resources to a cause in which one believes or the joy of achieving the immortality of personal influence because we cared enough to share and determine, at least in a small way, the course of the future.

Not only should everyone have a will but they should also be sure that its bequests are current and represent their best thoughts and concerns in a rapidly changing society, in view of rapidly changing motives and purposes.

There are hallmarks, or milestones, when wills should be rewritten, or codicils affixed, to govern the disposition of real and personal property. What are these hallmarks or milestones?

• *The Attainment of Maturity.* Frequently, we are under the impression that estate planning is for those of mature years facing life's sunset. Yet one in three of us will not attain the age of 65 years. Incidents of mortality among the young make front page news as accidents in the air and on land and sea take their toll. Few such persons are without capital worth. Estate planning should begin in the high school years, as young people come to the time of life when they can make withdrawals from savings accounts without parental endorsement and can hold title to property. A simple will can facilitate fiscal procedures should tragedy befall.

• *Marriage.* Premarital counseling has become an accepted part of our lives. Hardly a marriage occurs in which couples are not advised concerning their privileges and rights, obligations and opportunities, problems and needs. Sexual compatibility is universally included in the sex-counseling package. Yet all examination of the pastoral counseling curricula of seventeen theological seminaries did not uncover a single one that included estate planning as a part of the premarital counseling package. Inasmuch as partners in marriage do not normally die at the same time, it is imperative that marriage partners have their own individual wills.

• *Purchases or Changes in Property.* A will, properly drawn, will include a legal description of real property to be distributed under its terms. Such a will should be revised each time property is acquired, disposed of, or changed. It should not be assumed that additional property acquired in subsequent years is automatically covered by the original will, even though two pieces of property may be contiguous. This may or may not be so. No property acquisition or disposition should be made without a careful review of the resulting implications in the will.

- *Child Bearing or Adopting Children.* Wills should be revised each time the family is enlarged either by birth or by adoption. Each child should be named in a will, and when a child marries, the married name should be included in the will as well as the given name. Divorce actions and the remarriage of siblings should activate a caution signal that it is time to review and perhaps revise one's will.

- *When Dependents Leave the Nest.* Usually, parents sense a greater responsibility for family members dependent upon them than for those who have attained maturity, have all of their faculties, and are economically independent. As family members leave the nest and the degree of dependency changes, revision of the will may be prudent.

- *Natural or Legal Separation.* One of every three marriages ends in divorce. Add to this alarming figure those that never reach a divorce court but come to legal separation as emerging patterns of cohabitation reduce social pressure on couples to formalize their new relationships with a legal ceremony. When a spouse expires or a marriage dissolves, it is most important that the will be revised, rewritten, or replaced.

- *Remarriage.* A second marriage may include children from previous marriages, and these will be important to one's consideration in determining the distribution of assets according to personal interests when death comes.

- *Priorities Change.* A will represents the best interests of an individual and reflects personal hopes and dreams. Priorities change with times and circumstances. In a voluntary society, interests and involvement in voluntary organizations and associations change as well. The will reflects the priorities and the degree of interest in family life, community organization, and systemic change. If for no other reason, a will should be reviewed systematically and carefully every five years.

- *Interests and Concerns Modify.* The will reflects one's interests and concerns as well as one's priorities. Priorities will figure largely in the disposition of one's real and personal property and assets, but other interests and concerns are evident in each life and deserving of consideration in will planning.

- *Obligations and Responsibilities.* Obligations and responsibilities often extend beyond family and organizational structures in this complex society of ours, and business and professional obligations and responsibilities often loom large for those upon whom many depend because of positions they hold. In these events, such persons will want history to record integrity and responsibility in these areas.

- *Relocation.* We are a mobile society. One in five families will move this year. The average family moves once in five years. While many will move within a principality, most will move across, state lines, where statutes will be different from those governing the will of an individual written to conform to the statutes in the state in which the will is drawn. It is most important that the will be reviewed carefully to ensure a valid document in every detail should death occur.

- *Independence Shifts to Dependence.* Often care is taken that dependents be provided for in wills when children are born or adopted and wills reviewed again when the nest empties as dependents become independent and self-reliant. There are times, however, when folk move from independence to dependence, and from dependence to independence again. Such situations should be reflected in the will. There are times when children may become dependent because of sickness or tragedy. Parents, too, may reach a time when assets are exhausted, and we want to provide more adequately for them, not because we are required to but because we care enough to provide the best possible within our means.

- *Required Changes in Guardianships, Trusteeships, and Executorships.* While these are not common and perhaps will not apply to one in twenty family situations, they are important in those situations where they do occur, and modification must be made to accommodate those changes as they become necessary. Designated guadians, trustees, or executors may die, become incapable, or relocate to places where it is not reasonable, logical, or economically feasible for them to serve. In those events, wise planning must be evident in the last will and testament.

In a sense, our last will and testament will reflect our responsibilities, concerns, and interests. These may indeed interweave, but many times responsibilities preclude interests, and at other times interests may preclude responsibilities. We oversimplify the nature of life when we assume that responsibilities, causes, and interests are one and the same. They simply are not. In a will, a person may well give priority to one over another, which is a privilege that life itself does not always afford. We are caught so much in the chain of circumstances that we become creatures of circumstance and not masters of fate. The drawing of a will offers us an opportunity to choose as we wish and to give expression to programs, devices, and interests dear to our hearts.

At no time and in no place is one required to use or employ legal counsel. A will that is properly drawn and signed in the presence of two witnesses is adequate. The terms of a will may be inconsistent with statutes, however. In such a circumstance, the will of the state takes precedence over a last will and testament of an individual. Therefore, the terms of a will should be consistent with the minimum provisions required by the state. Conformity to minimum terms of laws and statutes protects an individual's rights and privileges and does not inhibit or limit those rights and privileges. Legal consultation permits the individual to "write his own" without running the risk that an uninformed use of terms or designations may nullify the document and necessitate arbitrary litigation through long and expensive legal processes.

Qualified legal counsel can provide advice concerning tax implications in planning one's last will and testament to assist the individual to gain the greatest advantage possible to the estate, to one's heirs, and to the organizations and institutions he may want to include.

When preparing the will, one should keep in mind the question: What is the taxable estate? The taxable estate is the amount to which estate tax rates apply and includes all property included in the gross estate, less funeral and administration expenses, debts, and charitable contributions. Table 6 lists federal estate taxes.

Willing funds to qualified religious and charitable organizations reduces estate taxes. While bequests are made primarily for the benefit of the institution included in one's will, nevertheless, estate tax savings reduce the cost of the gift and may enable one to give far more than may have been thought possible. The estate tax deduction for charitable gifts is unlimited. The charitable gift is deductible from the estate in full before the estate tax rates apply.

TABLE 6. FEDERAL ESTATE TAXES

TAXABLE ESTATE (in dollars in excess of exclusion)		TAX (in dollars)		
from	to	base amount	this plus %age of	amount over
0	10,000	0	18	0
10,000	20,000	1,800	20	10,000
20,000	40,000	3,800	22	20,000
40,000	60,000	8,200	24	40,000
60,000	80,000	13,000	26	60,000
80,000	100,000	18,200	28	80,000
100,000	150,000	23,800	30	100,000
150,000	250,000	38,800	32	150,000
250,000	500,000	70,800	34	250,000
500,000	750,000	155,800	37	500,000
750,000	1,000,000	248,300	39	750,000
1,000,000	1,250,000	345,800	41	1,000,000
1,250,000	1,500,000	555,800	43	1,250,000
2,000,000	2,000,000	780,800	45	1,500,000
2,500,000	2,500,000	1,025,800	49	2,000,000
3,000,000	3,000,000	1,290,800	53	2,500,000
3,500,000	4,000,000	1,575,800	57	3,000,000
4,000,000 +		1,880,800	65	4,000,000

In some cases, it may be wise to provide direct grants to family members and friends. In other cases, it may prove much wiser to place property and money in trust for those we love. The income, and in some cases and under some circumstances the capital as well, may provide benefit to those we love as long as their needs exist. Then, when the terms of the trust are satisfied, the remainder will have been designated to religious or charitable institutions or organizations as referred to in the chapter dealing with Charitable Remainder Trusts.

Designation in estate planning certainly does not need to be confined to charitable organizations. Many organizations, institutions, and causes deserving of support do not qualify as charitable organizations under the Internal Revenue Code as defined in Section 501(c)(3). They need not be eliminated, but tax implications may be such that one may want to assess carefully the causes to benefit from one's final act of philanthropy and the means whereby they may receive the greatest benefit from one's charitableness.

Institutions and organizations may be included in a last will and testament in one of four categories:
- The General and Undesignated Bequest. In the general or undesignated bequest, the use of the assets so designated is left to the discretion of the trustees of the organization or institution.
- The Designated Bequest. In a designated bequest, the trustees of the organization or institution are limited to the use of the asset as defined by the terms of the last will and testament.
- The General and Undesignated Devise. In the general or undesignated devise, the use or disposition of the property designated is left to the discretion of the trustees of the organization or institution.

A form for the general or undesignated bequest or devise may read as follows:

I give and bequeath (or devise) to

_____
(name of organization)

incorporated _____(date)_____ in the State of

_____ ,
(name of state)

_____
(amount if bequest, description of property if devise)
for the general purposes of its work.

A form for the designated bequest or devise may read as follows:

_____
(name of organization)

incorporated _____(date)_____ in the State of

_____ ,
(name of state)

_____
(amount if bequest, description of property if devise)
to be used for: _____(indicate purpose)_____ .

- The Designated Devise. In the designated devise, the use or disposition of the property is defined by the last will and testament and reverts to the estate in the event that the trustees of the organizations or institution do not choose to abide by the terms of the devise.

In the event of a designated bequest or devise, it is wise to define the programmatic concern of the individual rather than the departmental structure of an organization or institution. As an illustration: The Presbyterian Church (U.S.A.) like many denominations and agencies, has gone through mergers and restructure. Some years ago, one may have designated a bequest to a particular type of children's work under the Board of Christian Education. There is now no Board of Christian Education in that denomination, and all children's work, whether educational or relief, is incorporated in a Program Agency. If a bequest is designated to educate children in migrant, refugee, or displaced situations, the designation is not contingent upon a particular structure or departmental designation. Designations should be specific enough to carry out the donor's interest but broad enough to give an agency the opportunity to carry out its activities in terms of its charter and mandate. Over the long term, we would do well to think of program rather than project, to think of agency rather than department, to think of cause rather than situation.

Two questions are paramount in will and bequest planning. *First*, what are one's primary responsibilities? *Second*, what is one's ultimate intent? Certainly, the average person has responsibility for those dependent upon him. An ultimate interest may be an alma mater. Gifts in trust can combine the assumption of primary responsibility and the support of ultimate interest. Consider this illustration:

David Jones has an estate potential of $1,250,000. Taxes on such an estate would total $192,800 at his demise. If the total estate were to pass to his daughter, the eventual taxes on her estate would total an additional $136,828. If David Jones establishes two trusts, he can increase his daughter's security and reduce the tax burden on both estates. One-half of his estate may be placed in trust for his daughter with the disposition of the remainder to be made by his daughter. One-half of his estate may be placed in trust for his daughter with the remainder going to his church and alma mater. The federal tax on his estate, as well as that of his daughter's, would be eliminated, thus saving as much as $329,628 in federal estate taxes.

Legal counsel should provide alternatives for selection and ensure protection of the best interests of the individual, the family, and the institutions to be included in estate planning.

Here the individual is in total control to design a last will and testament creative in giving, supporting causes and ideals projecting into the future as a part of one's personal immortality.

12

Computer Giving—
The Face of the Future

We need not look far back into history to see barter systems or re-
muneration through gifts-in-kind. Monetary systems emerged with
the urbanization of society, and coin of the realm became the medium for exchange when individuals and families had no more milk,
butter, or eggs with which to purchase tents, garments, or fuel.
Travel to remote areas in the world today, and in rural primitive
complexes one sees goods-in-kind not only acceptable but often
preferred. "After all," a native in South Sumatra said to me, "you
cannot eat coins and paper."

In little more than a half century, our society moved almost
universally from the barter system to the monetary system, and the
monetary system has emerged as an economy of credits and debits
as extended payment procedures put two chickens in almost every
pot and two cars in almost every garage. Industry hummed as deferred payments became ordinary, and many over extended themselves. Society moved into two camps, namely, the cash society and
the cashless society.

"I can get it wholesale!" were the key words as the rich became
richer and the poor remained poor and became poorer. Those who
could pay cash received handsome discounts as a reward for cash
procedures, while those who required time for payment paid more
and more for less and less. As the economy worsened, it became less
desirable for individuals to carry cash, to handle cash, and to make
cash purchases. As a result, many gained more by sustaining sizable

balances in investments than they could gain by putting hard cash on the line. And we became a check-writing society. At the same time our society moved in this direction, tax needs also increased, and wage and salary deductions ranging from income tax to property tax, from social security to medical care, became a part of our way of life. Withholding processes expanded to include such non-governmental functions as health insurance, union dues, retirement annuities, life insurance, credit union share purchases and payment obligations, savings bonds, pooled investments, and contributions to the United Way. The average employer today is faced with an average of twenty-seven possible programmed deductions. At the beginning of the fifth score of the twentieth century, the average wage earner is handling only 43 percent of earnings in a cash-flow manner.

Now plastic currency takes precedence over the checkbook and currency exchange as computer processes become increasingly sophisticated. So much so, in fact, that the Federal Reserve System estimates that we will come to the end of the check-writing period of American history within a decade. And almost before we are aware of what is happening, we will move to more sophisticated plastic currency in the form of the "smart card" to the computerized system of credits and debits dependent only upon electronic impulses.

Really? In April 1985, 18,371,000 persons receiving Social Security Benefits had authorized payment through DIRECT DEPOSIT. This is 40 percent of the 45,892,836 persons eligible for benefits. New authorizations are made each month. Over 50,000,000 persons in the United States receiving payments from government will do so through computer processes that debit accounts of the federal and state treasuries and credit accounts of government employees and recipients of Social Security. In 1984 the Department of Health and Welfare selected two communities in Michigan in which persons eligible for food stamps received a plastic card, termed by most the "smart card," incorporating a chip wherein the monthly credit was applied at a local banking institution. Debits, by vendors, were made against the chip as purchases were made. It is likely that the system will be introduced nationally in the very near future.

These give introduction to a new age of credits to personal accounts and debits against the same, programmed through computer processes to fulfill the obligations of the individuals concerned for taxes, lodging, food, transportation, medical and dental services, utilities, and the thousand and one things that make up the economic processes of this century of progress.

How will the system work?

The system will be uniform of necessity, but there will be several levels of computer consciousness. One will be the level of governmental control. A second level will be that of individually programmed processes. The third will be the level of consumer incentive. Let us look at them one at a time.

The first level of computer consciousness, governmental control, begins with infancy and continues until death—beyond death, in fact, inasmuch as it includes the terminal grant toward funeral expenses. The key index is the Social Security number, and the process will ensure support from birth, through infancy, youth, and the preparatory years; guarantee a minimum person-family income through the so-called productive years; and ensure minimum base support throughout the retirement years. Along the way, government will not only ensure minimum needs and income but will also prove responsible for our disabilities and eventualities. The entire system will be programmed by the legislative branch of government, executed by the executive branch of government, and assured by the judicial branch of government to be equitable and just. Some will respond by saying that this is impossible. But a view of our government processes today will convince them that we are practically there already.

The second level of computer consciousness, individually programmed processes, will be implemented by individuals or groups of individuals as authorizations are given for contracted computerized processes for the purchase of additional insurance, securities, automobiles, boats, trailers, and homes. Lines of credit will be governed by lending insitutions according to age, sex, education, and vocational expertise, which will govern the type of home, the size of car, the amount that we can purchase through processes assessed against future expectation, and as each contract is signed, authorizations are instituted to program these obligations against personal accounts for credit to corporate accounts as payments for commodities and services.

The third level of computer consciousness, consumer incentive, consists of the types of transactions that ordinarily are a part of consumer buying presently processed through deferred-payment accounts, open accounts, credit-card purchases, and bank-card processes. The thirty-day charge, the ninety-day account, and the twelve or twenty-four-payment plan, in terms of the level of obligation, constitute a sizable portion of the gross national product and sums for which individuals and families are responsible in the ordering of their economic processes.

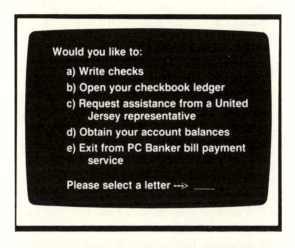

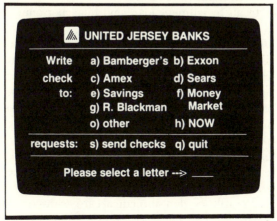

The menu for services and payments provided by United Jersey Banks.

Currently the United Jersey Banks has introduced its customers to an amazing information system that links a customer's personal home computer to the bank's high-speed computer when the computer number is dialed on the customer's telephone. Once the computer answers, the customer's bank account number and Personal Identification Number is automatically entered and five valuable services are instantly available:

• *Bill Payments.* Programmed into the bank's computer system are the customer's account numbers at merchants, utilities, or other third parties that the customer may wish to pay.

Each merchant is assigned a payment code, which is known only to the bank and the customer. Whenever the customer wishes to make payment, a command is entered into his personal computer with the amount to be paid.

A payment can be scheduled up to 30 days in advance, or instructions can be given to the bank to send the payment every month for the same amount.

• *Balance Inquiry.* Customers can contact the bank's computer 24 hours a day to determine the balance on their checking or savings account. Further, the amounts due on loans and current rates on certificates of deposit are available whenever the customer requests.

• *Funds Transfer.* The customer also can give instructions to the bank using their personal computer to transfer funds between United Jersey accounts. For instance, customers can make monthly payments to an installment loan, mortage, personal credit line, or IRA.

• *Checkbook Ledger.* All payments processed through electronic bill payments or funds transfer are automatically entered into the checkbook ledger. In addition, paper checks and deposits can be entered into the checkbook ledger in order to keep the electronic checkbook complete. The balances in the customer's account are automatically calculated when electronic payments or any direct entries are entered.

• *Updating Family Budget.* Having completed bill payments, the Home Information System may then be used to update the family budget. Each payment is entered with a payment type such as food, housing, utilities, dental/medical care, transportation, clothing, and insurance. Whenever necessary, the customer can view his actual payments against the family budget initially programmed into the system. The system in budget control is not limited to payments completed through the personal computer system. Cash transactions as well as other funds transfers may be fed into the computer for transaction memory retention and recall purposes.

Future services by United Jersey Banks, reported by Michael J. Dunn, Assistant Vice-President and Manager of the Electronic Funds Transfer Systems, will include home financial management in which customers can apply for certificates of deposit or personal loans directly from their home. Also, the customer will be able to view his checking account activity at his home computer. This information will include check numbers, amounts, and descriptions of items paid by the bank.

What does all this mean for our personal philanthropy? Computer processes will influence charitable giving in four ways:

First, computer processes will make for fewer contributions. While the computer system is convenient and efficient, it is also expensive. When computer time is contracted for one hundred minutes a month, little time is going to be given to processes that are not absolutely necessary. Contributions to 178 institutions or agencies will certainly become a thing of the past. Contributions to a single institution on a weekly basis will certainly become a thing of the past.

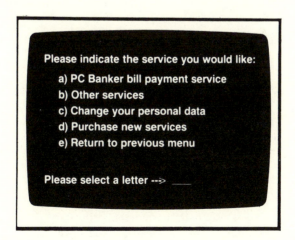

The menu for service selection in United Jersey Banks.

Second, computer processes will make for larger contributions. Many individuals will consider their giving in terms of their financial capability to give as budget procedures are built into the computer system and these processes make the tax implications more plainly evident.

How much does it cost you to give the money you give? The following table will be helpful in determining the cost of your gifts in terms of your taxable income and the benefit of charitable deductions:

TABLE 7. TAX BENEFITS OF CHARITABLE CONTRIBUTIONS

Taxable income (in dollars)	Net cost of $1 gift		
	Married couple filing jointly	Single	Head of household
$ 1,000	$ 0.86	$ 0.85	$ 0.86
2,000	0.85	0.83	0.84
4,000	0.83	0.81	0.82
8,000	0.81	0.76	0.78
12,000	0.78	0.73	0.75
16,000	0.75	0.69	0.72
20,000	0.72	0.64	0.68
32,000	0.61	0.55	0.58
44,000	0.52	0.50	0.50
50,000 +	0.50	0.50	0.50

This table shows the actual cost to the contributor after taking federal tax deductions into account. State and city income taxes further increase the after-tax value of donations and so actually reduce even more the net cost to the contributor.

We, as American people, have a lot to give. In the past, we have also tended to give often. And frequency of giving has tended to exaggerate or magnify the amount we give in our own thinking. One may give to a church fifty-two times a year, but when one's giving each time is only a dime, quarter, fifty cents, or dollar, the total giving is modest even in terms of the poverty level in our economy. With computer consciousness, the amount we give will become the important factor over and above the times we give or the number of contributions we make.

Third, there will be fewer appeals for charitable dollars and a greater consolidation in structures for philanthropy. Organizations that seem to thrive on small contributions, namely one, two, five, and ten dollar bills, will simply be unable to do so as the cost of securing the gift may well exceed the value of the gift. Therefore, it will be necessary that like causes merge to increase their capability and at the same time reduce their administrative and developmental costs over and against the sums they receive. We should be assured of better services through the funding we provide.

Fourth, our giving will be programmed into budget processes that provide a regularity and consistency of support that will lend efficiency to philanthropic organizations by eliminating the highs and lows in cash flow. In the United States, more than half of our philanthropic dollars move from the private sector to the charitable sector in the last twenty-five days and the first seven days of the calendar year. The expense of financing institutions and organizations with year-end income is one of the absurdities of our philanthropic system today. It is inexcusable in terms of the capability of the American people in this twentieth-century society. The strength of the United Way, and the genius of its operation, rests in its ability to control cash flow and provide fiscal integrity to institutions through the payroll deduction, or withholding, process for wage earners.

A wariness of computer giving lies in our fear of impersonal relationships between donors and the receiving organizations or institutions. In this respect, we must remember that the computer process is only the medium through which funds transfers are made. This is no different from mailing a check or programming a pledge through banking processes as far as personal relations are concerned. Whether our procedures utilize money, checks, or computerized credits and debits, the end result is still people giving to people, folk sharing in deserving causes, individuals contributing to the well being of others. The medium for sharing is not the end but a means to the end, and we should not lose sight of this. The medium is not as important as the cause, but the medium increases in importance as the cause gains in benefits resulting from our use of a more astute system.

The National Consultation on Financial Development has developed AUTOGIVE, whereby individuals may make monthly contributions to nonprofit agencies. The agency selects the fifth or twentieth day of the month for electronic funds transfers authorized by donors from their banking accounts to the bank account of the agency. The cost to the agency is twenty cents per transaction. Currently local churches participating in the program are receiving approximately twenty percent of their income from such authorizations. Headquarters for the National Consultation on Financial Development are located at 31 Langerfeld Road in Hillsdale, N.J., 07642 (201 664-8890).

We will tend to become more creative in our giving as we limit the number of our gifts, increase the size of our gifts, program our giving with regularity, and insist that change and improvement become products of our giving.

13

Creative Giving

In Chapter 12, we suggested that four things would result from computer processes as they relate to philanthropy. *First*, computer processes will make for fewer contributions. *Second*, computer processes will make for larger contributions. *Third*, computer processes will make for fewer appeals for charitable dollars and a greater consolidation in structures for philanthropic services. *Fourth*, computer processes will cause much giving to be programmed through budget processes, providing a regularity and consistency of support that will tend toward greater economy and efficiency in philanthropic organizations. These all will provide a good foundation for creative giving.

One of the discoveries we have made is that much of what we intend as philanthropy never truly becomes philanthropy at all. Development and processing costs are such that it is not unusual to find organizations and agencies simply raising money to raise money to survive. Few donors consider their gifts in terms of the value of the actual service resulting from their gifts. A gift seems justified for most in terms of the cause for which the organization has been chartered. It is valid to assume that for most organizations dependent upon mail solicitation, where the average gift is under $10, the development costs alone, in terms of literature, postage, and administration, may require between 60 and 80 percent of the gift. The more particular the service defined, the more costly the process. This is inevitable. As we view the horizon of philanthropy, it is difficult to justify what we do. Nevertheless, even in situations where only 20 percent goes to actual services in meeting human needs, we tend to believe that the end indeed does justify the means.

What is the matter here? Our first assumption is that the fault lies in the institution or organization. Yet if they were not organized, did not interpret or promote the cause, and did not provide the services for which they were chartered, it is entirely possible that nothing would be done at all in their particular area of concern and expertise. In addition, it takes only a little discussion with organization presidents and executive directors to learn that they, too, are distressed that development, processing, and administrative costs are so great. Wherein is the fault then? Actually, the fault is in the donor. Our patterns of giving provide a matrix for exorbitant costs.

Indeed, as we have analyzed the ways in which we give, we have found that our list of charitable contributions probably falls into two categories, namely, the person to person and the person to institution. The greatest percentage of a contribution goes to meet human need in the person-to-person situation unless it is actually a rip-off and the game plan is not truly honest from the outset. A case in point would be when an individual seeks your direct support to assist a needy family and upon receiving your gift goes to an off-track betting parlor and plays your money on the horses. If the effort is legitimate, the money passes directly from you through the solicitor to the family in need. Development costs when contributions flow from donors through institutions to meet human needs range from 3 to 80 percent—and actually, in some few and isolated cases, the entire amount. We have alluded to these previously.

Moreover, we have discovered that when we analyze our contributions in terms of their size, it becomes apparent that much of our giving goes not to support a cause at all but to support an institution. Organizations whose development costs are modest, perhaps 3 to 20 percent, would qualify among those where gifts support the cause. Those whose development costs may range from 60 to 100 percent would qualify among those where gifts support an institution. In the latter case, while there is indeed value in interpretation and communication, the gift simply cannot deliver actual services in meeting or arresting human need. Gifts usually are not capable of doing so unless they exceed $14.69. It is for this reason that I state that sums under $14.69 support the institution, while sums exceeding $14.69 tend to support the cause.

Even worse, we have learned that some of our largest total gifts are made up of many small contributions and gifts, as in the case of a local church. Payments may be made as often as fifty-two or more times in the course of a year. Here, because of the proximity of the individual to the institution, the development cost per contribution, or transaction, will not be as costly as for other organizations; however, it will not be as modest, cost-wise, as for a single contribution equal to the annual gift. The more numerous the payments, the more costly the process in the course of a year. Fifty-two gifts in a year will require greater administrative and processing costs than a single contribution. It would not be unusual however, to discover that the cost of the fifty-two-process procedure would require one-third of the funding, and the cost of twelve processes one-fifth of the funding. Thus, the movement by financial structures in charitable and religious organizations from the weekly and monthly processes to the quarterly process is a move in the right direction.

The dividing line between the causes we support programmatically and the causes we support institutionally will tend to fall at about the 75 percentage line in our list. In other words, 25 percent of the organizations to which we contribute receive gifts of such size and proportion that they meet, at least in part, the programmatic and service function of a donor's expectancy. Seventy-five percent of them will not—except in those cases where the contribution is a person-to-person type.

Upon discovering this, we will tend to bring causes into focus and to concentrate on particular programs and projects that challenge interest, stimulate response, and encourage support. We will tend to select particular programs and causes for major support as well as minor support; programs and causes that we will support in the short term and those that we will support over a long term. The tendency will be toward significant support with charitable dollars, the development of primary and secondary interests and causes challenging meaningful support as expressions of our deepest concerns in not only immediate support but in the areas of deferred giving and estate planning.

As we view our lists, there will emerge two or three causes in the primary group that will demand our attention and major support.

Each will challenge us to form a module that will include one, two, or three phases. The first phase is that of immediate funding. The second phase is in terms of short-term funding. The third phase is in terms of long-range planning that may include deferred giving, wills, and bequests. If we select three in this category, it is not likely that all three will be of equal importance or receive the same attention and support. We will tend to arrange them in order of our concerns, interests, and priorities, and the primary cause will be the one that will benefit most from our creative giving.

The primary cause will challenge our greatest support now and in the near future. The primary cause will challenge our support over a long term—perhaps the remainder of our lives. The primary cause will become the focal point of our outreach and perhaps benefit from our personal longing for immortality as an expression that will extend beyond our years and preserve evidence of our interest, concern, and support.

The design, then, consists of immediate funding, longterm support, and major support through deferred giving. The first two aspects need little explanation. The third, however, may include some of the following:

• Deferred Payment Gift Annuities contracted at mid-life with income beginning at retirement or age 65.

• The establishment of a Charitable Remainder Unitrust providing for the maximum tax benefits at the time the trust is created and the avoidance of capital gains as the investment grows in the pooled portfolio of securities constituting the Unitrust.

• The establishment of a Living Revocable Trust as a modern and flexible financial and estate-planning tool providing hedges for inflation and estate taxes while preserving the option of utilization of capital should adverse market conditions or a family or personal situation require it.

• The establishment of a Charitable Remainder Trust assuring income annually beginning at age 65 with income related to market conditions and the fluctuation of the value of securities in trust.

• The establishment of the Charitable Remainder Annuity Trust providing fixed income beginning at age 65 and assuring a support base regardless of market or economic conditions.

• The assignment of insurance policies to charitable organizations or institutions, reducing the premium load required of an individual whose insurance needs decline. Such an assignment constitutes a charitable contribution for tax purposes.

- The preparation, or revision, of a will, including a devise or bequest designation to support our primary interest.

While some or all of these may be utilized to support our primary interest, we mentioned that out of the 25 percent receiving major support we might select three. Meaningful support may be designated to the two constituting secondary interests, and our support to one or two may continue over a period of time or receive a one-time gift of significant size.

Among the 75 percent of organizations receiving token support, creative giving would invite us to select three causes for which a somewhat significant gift could be made on a one-time basis or perhaps one gift a year spanning a number of years.

Significant support is a product of selection and concentration. Limiting the number of causes and consolidating gift values result in meaningful support.

To more fully understand the opportunities and advantages of creative giving, let us consider a brief overview of the lives of John and Jane Jones:

John and Jane were raised in similar communities and met during their college years. Both were products of mid-America, average families, and both shared in community opportunities for worship, recreation, and personal development illustrated by their church, the Scouting organizations, YW-YMCAs, and the dozens of organizations that cross community lines to produce upright citizens and moral people. Both families shared in the support of their churches and paid their dues to the various organizations to which they belonged. Both contributed reasonably to deserving causes as appeals were made to them.

In college, John majored in physics and chemistry, looking forward to a career in engineering. Jane looked forward to becoming a homemaker but felt that for cultural as well as personal reasons she would endeavor to meet the qualifications for certification in elementary education. She had no desire that this become a vocational adventure but felt that this type of education would be excellent insurance should her mate sometime become disabled or if she were to become a widow without adequate resources to care for whatever family they might have.

John and Jane were married when they completed their formal education, and both secured positions that provided reasonably well for them. John's firm had a pension plan that would supplement Social Security benefits, and Jane qualified for the teacher's retirement plan as well.

They joined a church. John became a Boy Scout leader, and Jane became interested and active in the Junior League and the League of Women Voters. At the end of their first year of marriage, they reviewed their economic situation and discovered that while they had a reasonably good income they had saved practically nothing. Their itemized deductions consisted of contributions to twenty-seven organizations ranging from $104 to their church to $1 for the Society for Crippled Children. Their total giving was $278. They had entered into contracts for two life insurance policies, one on John's life for $25,000 and one on Jane's life for $10,000.

In the second year of their marriage, their church was moving into a building program, and they decided to match their giving for the new building, and so their giving over the next year to their church increased from $104 to $208. The YWCA was engaged in a refurbishing program, and they pledged $150 for that over a period of three years. At the conclusion of their second year, they had contributed to thirty-six organizations, and their contributions totaled $516.

As years passed, giving increased, programmed investments began to accumulate, and additional life insurance was purchased to provide not only for eventualities but also to meet the educational needs of their children as they approached college age. In the course of six years, they had three children, and with a change of positions and advancement, John's salary more than covered the loss of Jane's income when she became a full-time homemaker.

After ten years of married life, they discovered that they were contributing $4,000 a year to about forty organizations. Their church was receiving about 25 percent of their giving, and the remainder of their contributions were not of great significance or of great importance either to them or to the organizations to which they contributed.

In reviewing their contributions, as well as their interests, they decided to move into modular living. They made a list of the forty organizations to which they were giving and the amount they had contributed to each, with the organization receiving the largest sum at the top and those receiving the smallest sums at the bottom. They drew a line dividing the top ten and the bottom thirty. Those in the top ten received $3,650 over the course of the preceding twelve months. The other thirty received $350.

They focused their attention on the organizations in the top ten of their listing. Fifty percent had been given to their church and 25 percent to two other institutions. The remaining 25 percent was spread over seven organizations. They were convinced that two of the three should prompt a lifetime interest and that the third would receive support over the following three years, at which time it might be replaced by another organization. In reviewing the thirty causes receiving $350, they selected three; two to receive gifts of $150 each and one to receive a gift of $50. These, at that time, were considered one-time gifts.

Their church offered the opportunity for donors to pre-authorize their giving through AUTOGIVE whereby their monthly contribution would be debited against their checking account on the twentieth day of each month. They welcomed this means of ensuring regular support when frequently they were worshipping in distant places far from home.

Over the next five years, John had unusually fine increases in salary and was determined to reduce his tax load and at the same time increase his support to charitable organizations. In discussing the matter with his college's development officer, he discovered that he could invest $25,000 in a Deferred Payment Gift Annuity that would provide a good return at age 60 and at the same time provide an immediate gift value for tax purposes. As he did this, John and Jane's charitable contributions for the year more than doubled the amount they had given to charitable causes the previous year.

During the next five years, John's income increased greatly. He explored opportunities for establishing a trust but was hesitant to establish a Charitable Remainder Trust inasmuch as he could not be certain of his future and was determined to provide well for his spouse and children. With this in mind, he established a Living Revocable trust with $250,000. The trust would continue through both John's and Jane's lifetimes, provide substantial income annually to both or to the remaining spouse, and provide annual income to the three children until the youngest child attained maturity, in the event of their demise, at which time the funds in trust would be divided equally among them.

AUTOGIVE IS . . .

MAY

   WE

      SUGGEST . . . .

- A banking process whereby donors may order their church commitment paid automatically by their bank.

- A thoughtful action by responsible Christians who want to assure ministry and mission through regular, systematic giving.

- Convenient for donors - - no checks to write or mail.

. . . . AUTOGIVE

- Helpful in reducing administrative expense while assuring support even when you must be away, weather threatens or illness strikes.

- Easy to use. Merely complete the simple form and we'll do the rest.

- Safely regulated by banking laws. You may terminate participation at any time.

a thoughtful tool of
Christian Philanthropy
for the 2lst Century.

- Now used by thousands and available to you in making your church commitment even more helpful.

Four-panel information and authorization form for AUTOGIVE.

AUTHORIZATION FORM

I hereby authorize my bank to charge my account each month and pay the Church the amount shown in accordance with the conditions on the reserve side of this form.

Monthly Amount: $ _____

Date: _____

Signature: _____

Address: _____

City/State/Zip: _____

ATTACH A CHECK MARKED 'VOID' FOR THE ACCOUNT TO BE DEBITED EACH MONTH.

Your account will be debited on the 20th day of each month.

Mail this form to the Church Office. A copy will be returned to you.

AUTOGIVE CONDITIONS

This authorization to charge my account shall be the same as if I personally signed a check to the church.

A record of my payment will be included in my bank statement. This record will serve as my receipt.

I have the right to authorize my bank to reverse any erroneous entry. This must be done by written notice within 15 days of the date of the bank statement or within 45 days after the debit was made.

I may terminate my participation in this process upon written notification to the church.

All information is strictly confidential.

WOODLAND HILLS
COMMUNITY CHURCH
21338 Dumetz Road
Woodland Hills, CA 91364
346-0820

He was next approached by a college development officer and encouraged to consider a Charitable Remainder Trust with one-half of the residual going to Jane at the time of his death and the other half to their alma mater. They decided on an Annuity Trust at this time that would provide a fixed annual return for as long as either of them lived. Subsequently, they established a second Charitable Remainder Trust with their alma mater that would provide income based on the market value of the securities held in trust on the anniversary of the agreement. They were optimistic for the future and believed that they would likely bypass capital gains, as the securities in trust gained substantially in worth beyond the 6 percent income they would receive each year for as long as either of them lived.

John and Jane had received a substantial inheritance at the time of Jane's mother's demise, and they had invested it wisely in growth securities. Over the years, the securities had more than tripled in value, and it seemed wise to dispose of them, as prospects for the future were not very good. Yet if they were to sell the securities, they would face a sizable tax burden for capital gains. They discussed the situation with their pastor, who directed them to their denomination's foundation. At their suggestion, the securities were transferred to the foundation, thus avoiding all capital gains, and their invested shares were consolidated in the pooled investment portfolio of the denominational foundation as the means of establishing a Charitable Remainder Unitrust consisting of one thousand shares. They thereby avoided all capital gains and received a sizable tax deduction through the gift value of the securities used to establish the Unitrust.

During those years, their contributions to their local church had increased to $12,400 a year. When the new building was erected, there were facilities for a good program for youth on a weekday basis, but the congregation's mortgage obligation was too great for it to provide both mortgage payments and program direction. John and Jane decided that this should be an important function in their church, too important a service to the community for the church to neglect. They presented a challenge to the church officers that over a period of three years they would provide $40,000 a year for this type of program if the members of the congregation would match their giving with new money. Members' commitments were forthcoming, and they had the exciting experience of seeing their church begin a new program that was in part, at least, the product of their lives as well as their money.

Arriving at the time of life when their children had completed their educations, selected their mates, and established homes, they turned their thoughts to more meaningful estate planning to determine how their fondest dreams could be fulfilled in the lives of others devoted to service in a degree, and in a capacity, that they were unable to do themselves. Reverting to the original compilation of causes to which they had contributed in a single year during the third year of their married life, they completed a list of the causes to which they had made significant gifts through the years. As they did so, they discovered that one cause to which they had contributed comparatively little was of importance to them. Their rather limited support was governed by their lack of knowledge of the organization and situation it served. In estate planning, they determined that three causes would benefit through grants at the demise of the surviving spouse. One-half of the estate would remain in trust, providing benefit for the surviving spouse, and at the time of the survivor's demise, the remainder of the trust would remain in trust for a period of twenty years, with each of the children benefiting from the trust in annual income. The children reserved the option of establishing new trusts or receiving the assets as remaindermen at the termination of the original trust. One gift was to be selected in cooperation with one of the three organizations receiving grants at the time of John's demise to establish a memorial for him, and one gift was to be selected among the three charitable organizations to establish a memorial to Jane at her demise. The other two gifts, in each instance, were to be unrestricted.

Three other developments occurred in their lifetimes. *First*, as the years went by, they entered into agreements with several organizations for Gift Annuities, reducing their tax burden by gift values and tax excluded income annually. *Second*, they assigned the title of their condominium to their church and reserved the right of occupancy for as long as they would be capable of residing in it. Sufficient funds were placed in escrow to insure the property, pay the taxes, and maintain the property in excellent condition. *Third*, in time, they reduced their insurance protection by making certain organizations and institutions the irrevocable beneficiaries of particular policies. In some cases, policies were retained by John and Jane with the payment of premiums qualifying as charitable contributions.

Through the last two decades of their lives together, authorization was made that funds be transferred from their bank accounts to the bank account of their church on a monthly basis to ensure support of the church in spite of irregular attendance resulting from age and infirmity.

Creative giving was the secret to fulfillment in John and Jane's lives and provides a key to creative philanthropic enterprises for each of us. Their experience provides a pattern for exercising discipline in giving and estate planning in an exciting, meaningful way, a pattern that will enable all of us to find joy through giving.

Index